Better Homes and Gardens®

Deck&Patio
PLANNER

Better Homes and Gardens® Books
Des Moines, Iowa

Better Homes and Gardens® Books
An imprint of Meredith® Books

Deck & Patio Planner
Editor: Paula Marshall
Writer: John Riha
Contributing Editor: Diane A. Witosky
Associate Art Director: Mick Schnepf
Designer: David Jordan
Copy Chief: Catherine Hamrick
Copy and Production Editor: Terri Fredrickson
Book Production Managers: Pam Kvitne, Marjorie J. Schenkelberg
Contributing Copy Editor: Jim Steppe
Contributing Proofreaders: Jean O. Ellis, Pam Wright, Raymond L Kast
Contributing Illustrators and Designers: Erich Lage, The Art Factory
Indexer: Kathleen Poole
Electronic Production Coordinator: Paula Forest
Editorial and Design Assistants: Kaye Chabot, Mary Lee Gavin, Karen Schirm

Meredith® Books
Editor in Chief: James D. Blume
Design Director: Matt Strelecki
Managing Editor: Gregory H. Kayko
Executive Shelter Editor: Denise L. Caringer

Director, Retail Sales and Marketing: Terry Unsworth
Director, Sales, Special Markets: Rita McMullen
Director, Sales, Premiums: Michael A. Peterson
Director, Sales, Retail: Tom Wierzbicki
Director, Book Marketing: Brad Elmitt
Director, Operations: George A. Susral
Director, Production: Douglas M. Johnston

Vice President, General Manager: Jamie L. Martin

Better Homes and Gardens® Magazine
Editor in Chief: Jean LemMon
Executive Building Editor: Joan McCloskey

Meredith Publishing Group
President, Publishing Group: Christopher M. Little
Vice President, Finance & Administration: Max Runciman

Meredith Corporation
Chairman and Chief Executive Officer: William T. Kerr

Chairman of the Executive Committee: E. T. Meredith III

Contents

Capture Your Dreams

Planning a deck or patio begins with imagining everything you want the space to be.

Cramped for space with a small urban lot, a St. Louis couple dreamed of an inviting flagstone patio. They realized that dream by installing a 700-square-foot patio over an existing flat-roofed garage. Increasing the number of ceiling joists in the garage helped carry the weight and covering the roof with a butyl rubber membrane prevented leaks.

Whether you work with a design professional on your project or create the look yourself, you're more likely to get what you want if you rely on your own imagination. Decks and patios open up to the sun, the sky, and nearby landscaping, and are especially fun projects because they encourage creativity. Even if your ideas seem farfetched, don't discard them. Who knows? A design professional might provide a clever solution that gives you just what you imagined.

We've talked with professional architects, landscape architects, and landscape designers from across the country about creating satisfying outdoor living spaces. Their ideas should inspire you to bring your own getaway dreams to life.

This first chapter taps the considerable professional experience of: Bruce Pierce, landscape designer, Des Moines; Dave Rolston, landscape architect, Dallas; Sarah Nettleton, AIA, Minneapolis; Linda Searl, FAIA, Chicago; Gene Kunit, landscape architect, Sebastopol, California; Matt Moynihan, landscape architect, St. Louis; Katherine Evans, landscape architect, Alameda, California.

ASSESSING YOUR FEELINGS

Below: This deck-and-patio combination is just right for after-work relaxing in the shade. Opposite: A raised platform deck brings a touch of Asian lifestyle to rural Illinois. Opaque acrylic replaces traditional rice paper in the screen panels.

"Try approaching a project with a poetic heart: Why do you want to be outside? For more intimacy? For a change of pace? How do you want to feel when you're out there? Work through these bigger questions first, then move to the details.

"Some people want to re-create the dreamy feeling of swinging on the porch at Grandpa's; others want the noisy stimulation of a Parisian sidewalk cafe. To get what you really want, materials and construction have to follow the sensations and functions that you're after.

"American culture is a mix of many, so you can take influences from them all and make the garden space that you want. We're not locked into a singular national style, such as the Japanese or English are. For an 'anything goes' country—you've got it here."

CREATING STYLE AND HARMONY

"Railings, planters, trellises, and benches—the details of these elements can repeat and relate to those of the house. The architecture of a house can offer a lot of clues. Check rooflines and windowpanes for shapes and themes; scout architectural detailing, even fireplace surrounds."

—architect, Linda Searl, FAIA

"Work toward organizing your design around a focal point, a philosophy, maybe a pool or a fireplace. If you love birds, you can arrange a space around a birdbath. You can also work with a style, say modernism or a Mediterranean look. Just try to find a physical thing or a theme that you can latch onto and work with to make the design special. Go to your interests for a theme—what moves you—is it travel, gardening, or art? Let that drive the design of your outdoor space. Style trends will come and go, but if your space is designed with your passions in mind, it will be timeless. And if someone respects it later, it's still timeless.

"Try to think of the whole space; not just the deck details, but also the trees and gardens that will be part of the scene. I like to mix soft, casual plantings, such as ornamental grasses and artemisia, with more formally laid-out patios."

— landscape architect Dave Rolston

"You'll find design clues in the landscape where you live. Every region has its own palette of colors and textures, so go take a walk or a drive. The landscape will tell you what goes together."

— landscape architect Gene Kunit

Below: An unusual half-round deck adds a distinct style and character to the back of this small Minneapolis bungalow. Finely designed railings and posts are especially well-detailed.
Opposite: A simple circular patio defined by a low stone wall is the ideal complement to a backyard filled with greenery. The round table echoes the shape of the patio design.

FINDING A SITE TO BEHOLD

"In urban Chicago, where space is tight but people want to be outdoors, we'll use whatever usable space we can find! We've designed beautiful side-yard patios, rooftop decks, even a deck on top of a detached garage."

– *architect, Linda Searl, FAIA*

"Sometimes, the only and best location for a deck or patio is off the back of the house. There's nothing wrong with a single rectangle; done well, it can be quite elegant. But for placement, try wandering your property to find the spots that you enjoy. Go upstairs, look out the windows, and check out the rooftops, too. Then you can make notes about what you might like to do—get away for some reading here, gather with friends under the tree over there—and the design and placements will come together more easily."

– *landscape architect Katherine Evans*

"Outdoor spaces tended to be stiff entertaining places; but now, families want to use their whole yards for many different purposes. It's hard for one space to have 20 different personalities. Lots of people want a place to entertain outdoors, but also a place to blow off steam or listen to music, a place to talk with a friend, another place to feel secluded and quiet. You can get what you want, even on a small lot, by floating a series of spaces away from the house. These might be decks, patios, or a combination. Link them with paths or steps to create a sense of open flow, and blend them with swaths of plantings to soften and naturalize the effect. These spaces don't need to be large or grand—people often forget to create smaller scale, intimate spaces—but these are often the spaces they value the most in the end."

– *landscape architect Matt Moynihan*

Above: Set away from the main house and accessible by a flagstone path, surrounding trees and shrubs border this small, private patio. A latticework privacy fence screens views to nearby neighbors. **Opposite:** Taking advantage of vistas across the San Diego Bay, a rooftop patio features an arbor that lends a touch of Mediterranean style.

CHOOSING MATERIALS THOUGHTFULLY

Opposite: A large concrete urn is a graceful and elegant focal point when set in the middle of a meandering patio made with affordable pea gravel. Below: This thoughtfully composed deck-and-patio combination features two kinds of brick, wooden decking, a spa, and an unusual arbor. Generous garden plantings help harmonize the various elements.

"Tropical hardwoods such as Pau Lope have always been available, but there's been a big increase in its use for decking. These woods are exceptionally dense, rot- and bug-resistant, and are beautiful and long-lasting. The look is like that of a boat: very high quality"

– landscape architect Matt Moynihan

"Don't overlook pea gravel and decomposed granite. These affordable materials are big on charm, they can be mixed with other materials such as pavers or stepping stones, and can be an economical way to work out your patio."

– landscape architect Dave Rolston

"Of course, I like to use natural materials, but I see a revolution in the works with steel and plastics replacing wood for increasingly attractive building material options. It's a good way to go, and it's ecologically responsible.

"As for quarry products, the variety is better than ever. It doesn't matter where you live, you can get tile and slate from India, slate from China, stone from Oklahoma or Arizona. Transporting these materials has become commonplace in the market."

– landscape architect Gene Kunit

ATTENDING TO DETAILS

"For the most part, the opportunity to personalize a space is in the vertical details—the railings, benches, and planters. Material choices are especially vast for railings and trellises—you can combine wood or iron, pipe, Plexiglas, cattle fencing, even corrugated drainpipe."

– landscape designer Bruce Pierce

"Detail, scale, and proportion are what will distinguish a project more than anything else. For instance, if you choose a broad series of shallow, deep steps rather than the typical steep and narrow variety, your deck or terrace will have a more gracious, easy feel to it. In many cases, you'll eliminate the need for guardrails, too. What a boon; think about it, these rails often block your view when you're sitting down. And yet another broad step advantage: They boost your party seating capacity in a big way. Take that idea further: If there's an edge, sit on it! If you need a retaining wall, see if there's a way to work in a sitting ledge for even more seating possibilities!"

– landscape architect Katherine Evans

Opposite: An arched opening leads to a small projecting balcony on this stylish deck. The unusual two-tiered overhead rafter structure supports a canopy of wisteria and trumpet vines. Below: Ornamental fretwork made of lattice and a Chippendale-styled railing system are simple, elegant touches.

THINKING OF A DECK OR PATIO AS PART OF A WHOLE

Above: Painted wrought-iron railings and cut stone walkways enhance the gracious exterior of a traditional home. The covered eating area is located just off the dining room for alfresco meals.

"As you plan your outdoor space, consider its impact on the rest of your home. If the door to the deck is off the eating area, your eating area will soon become a hallway. You might want to make some adjustments indoors to accommodate this. Likewise, attached decks can block light from flowing into basement rooms. Maybe you don't care; if you do, you can build a beautiful design that pushes the structure away from the house and still allows shafts of light through the structure.

"Decks built over basement walkout rooms can look severe, and can also cut off the sun that's needed for patio plantings below. See if you can make things more interesting and grab more light by working angles into the picture. If you're laying a patio, can its shape be softened or enlarged or angled to complement what's above?

Left: A long, low platform deck complements the horizontal lines of a single-story, ranch-style house. The deck is close to the ground, so railings are not necessary. Potted plants add visual texture. Below: A rock garden and a patio with sweeping curves serve to draw the eye toward the house. The informal curves work well with this simple bungalow.

If you're building a retaining wall, can it come into the picture by way of a curve or angle?

"On an even more detailed note, remember storage. If you're going to keep a water garden out there, where will you keep your tools? Nifty storage areas can be tucked into corners, railings, and under decks."

— landscape designer Bruce Pierce

MAKING CONSCIENTIOUS CHOICES

"Sustainable design is an important part of my design work and is increasingly important to homeowners. How do we build what we're after without using more resources than necessary? You can start working responsibly when you tear off an existing project: Can framing material or other boards be reused? Send decimated wood to the chipper. If you have hulks of concrete to haul away, call a demolition company to pick it up and grind it into road fill. They can grind any asphalt shingles too. You might have to make a few phone calls to get this done, but you'll be doing something important—you'll be a hero!

"For your new structure, consider fabricated woods that weather out just like real wood and are less likely to rot. Or ask better lumber suppliers about the availability of reclaimed wood: fine quality wood that's been stripped from buildings and structures. Finally, ask for hardwoods raised in certified-sustainable forests rather than clear-cut forests. Sustainable forests—those in which trees are cut selectively rather than all at once—have even been proven to be more productive in the long run than clear-cut forests, and the big lumber companies are starting to catch on. The availability of these materials is increasing, so ask for it!"

— *architect Sarah Nettleton, AIA*

Below: The all-time favorite paving material—traditional red brick—is economical, durable, and comfortable to walk on. It comes in a variety of colors and styles, so it is relatively easy to match new brick to existing masonry. Opposite: Tropical ipe is a dense hardwood that is grown commercially in Brazil. Ipe has a rich, lustrous look that gives a deck the aura of fine furniture. Ipe must be specially ordered.

Evaluating Your Property

The shape and prominent features of your property can give character to the design of your project.

A fabulous garden is the star of this deck and patio project that includes wide stone steps leading to the yard. The homeowners can sit and admire their flowers and shrubs from a special seating nook with a stationary glider. Next to the house, open-air dining is just a few steps from the kitchen.

Decks and patios are outdoor rooms that have many of the components of traditional indoor living spaces—floors, furnishings, accessories, and sometimes even walls and ceilings. Despite these similarities, the shape, contours, and physical characteristics of your property are some of the most influential elements of your deck or patio design. Creating an outdoor living area that integrates the best attributes of your property—and avoids the worst—should be your primary goal.

As you begin to make your plans, take the time to get to know your property. Take photographs at different times of the day. Walk out into your yard and see where there is sun and shade. Check out the views, how close the neighbors are, and how traffic patterns lead to and from gardens, gates, and ancillary structures. Take notes about what works best and what doesn't. For example, you might notice that there is plenty of shade at the southwest corner of your property from 4 p.m. through the remainder of the evening—ideal conditions for summer entertaining. "Roughing in" the location of your deck or patio by "seeing" where it will be is an important first step toward an effective plan.

Four major physical characteristics affect the placement and configuration of a deck or patio—shape, slope, shade, and views. Prominent landscaping features, such as large rocks, big trees, and gardens, also can play key roles in determining how your deck or patio will be situated. Begin by creating a map of your property that identifies important physical characteristics. Once your map is complete, you can use it to help determine the location of your deck or patio.

Your property's shape

If your property is large, there probably are many possible locations for a deck or patio. You might have a choice between morning or evening sun, views to the south or east, and other considerations. If your house is on a modest suburban property or a smaller, narrow urban lot, your options are limited and you'll need to plan space carefully. To begin planning, start with a plat of your property: a map that shows your lot in relation to neighboring lots. It is available at your local planning and zoning offices, usually free of charge. The plat shows the size and shape of your lot, and it indicates the location of any easements—corridors established on your property that, by law, must be kept free of any structures or impediments. Here are four examples of easements:

■ *Utility easements* provide space so that crews can access electrical power lines or other utilities to make repairs. Utility easements often are at the rear of property lines and can run the length of the neighborhood. They are usually 5 to 10 feet wide.

■ *Overland flowage easements* include significant depressions or gullies that collect running water during downpours or when snow melts. These physical land characteristics must not be altered or blocked by construction. Flowage easements prohibit structures from being built close to runoff

Right: A typical plat map shows the location of your house and that of your immediate neighbors. Setbacks and easements are indicated by dashed lines. The additional lines on this map show that annexations—subtracting a strip of land from one lot and adding it to an adjacent property—have occurred routinely.

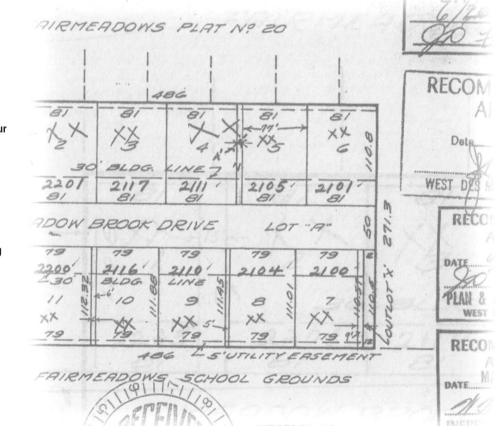

"Bathtub" patio

Drainpipe | Retaining wall | Catch basin

Slope

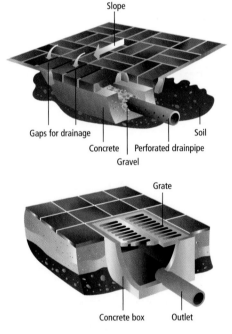

Gaps for drainage | Soil
Concrete | Perforated drainpipe
Gravel

Grate

Concrete box | Outlet

areas where foundations could be undermined or damaged.

■ *Accessibility easements* ensure a piece of property has direct access to a main road or byway. Creating these easements is a common practice when property is split into two parcels, creating a front-facing lot adjacent to a road and a rear-facing lot that is not. An accessibility easement usually ensures that there is enough space for a driveway to access the main road from the rear property.

■ *Buffer easements* are created when a piece of property is next to a public park. The buffer prevents residential construction from intruding too closely on the environment of the park.

In addition to easements, construction is subject to setbacks—distances measured from the edges of a piece of property. A typical suburban lot might have a front setback of 30 to 40 feet, side setbacks of 15 feet, and rear setbacks of 10 to 20 feet. New construction cannot take place in the setback.

You can use your plat to begin making your property map and, eventually, for your entire project (see Chapter 3, "Planning with a Purpose"). Copy your plat by hand or with a photocopier, and keep several copies to create variations of your design plans.

Slope

The contours of your property—how it rises and falls—often is summed up as "slope." The slope of your property determines if

you'll need excavation and grading work or a drainage system to carry runoff away from your foundation. Decks usually are less affected by slope because they can be built to vault over the changes in terrain. The design of a patio, however, can be dramatically affected by slope. If your property is flat, you'll have considerable freedom in the design and placement of a patio. Any noticeable slope, however, can be a primary consideration when designing your project.

To help visualize the slope, make a sketch of your property as seen from the side. Side views are called elevations. Your elevation should indicate the location of your

Providing adequate drainage is a primary consideration for backyards where the land slopes toward the house. A typical "bathtub" patio features a relatively flat area surrounded by a retaining wall. To prevent precipitation and snow melt from gathering in the patio, water is drained by perforated pipe buried in a gravel-filled trench. The pipe extends to a side yard where it exits the ground to let gravity carry the water beyond the house foundation.

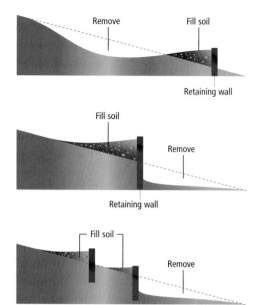

Right: With the help of retaining walls, land can be reshaped and flattened for a patio. Most methods call for moving—not removing—soil to sculpt flat areas. Severe slopes, or terraces, might require one or more retaining walls. Below: Nestled on a scenic hill, this house has few places for a patio. The owners used soil from the excavated basement to support a patio near the front entry.

house and how the surrounding property rises and falls. Take some simple measurements so you can draw your elevations as close as possible to scale.

Without using specialized equipment, such as a transit, your elevations will be an estimate of the slope. Although not very accurate, these sketches will be valuable planning tools. They also will be an important way to help communicate your ideas to an architect, builder, or other professionals involved in the construction of your project.

To create elevations for property that falls away from the house, stretch a string line from the base of your house foundation to a distance of about 20 feet. Two people make this task easier. Use a line level to

Determining slope

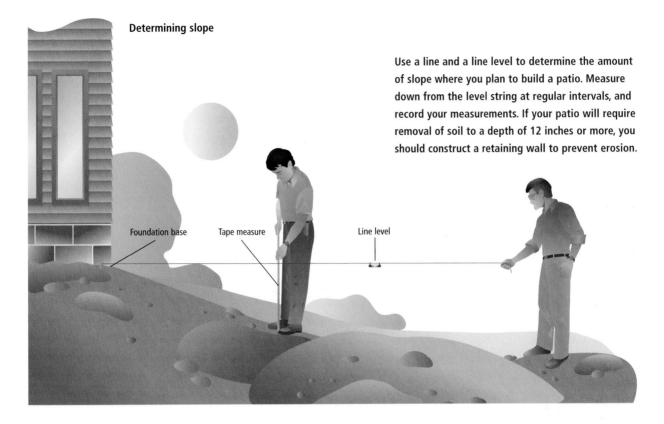

Use a line and a line level to determine the amount of slope where you plan to build a patio. Measure down from the level string at regular intervals, and record your measurements. If your patio will require removal of soil to a depth of 12 inches or more, you should construct a retaining wall to prevent erosion.

Foundation base   Tape measure   Line level

make sure the string is plane. Measure from the string to the ground every 5 feet, and record your findings on a sketch. If necessary, measure out another 20 feet, holding the string at the ground and extending it from the end of your previous measurement.

To create elevations for property that slopes toward a house, reverse the process. Begin at a point up the slope 20 feet away from the house, then pull the string to the house and establish a level line.

If the land slopes toward the house, then establishing a level location for a paved area probably will require a "bathtub" patio—a flat area surrounded by a retaining wall. Installing adequate drainage in a bathtub patio will prevent water from collecting in the "basin" of the "tub." Too much water in the soil can lead to leaky basements or settling of the foundation—problems that are costly to fix.

A drainage system, usually perforated drainpipe buried in gravel-filled trenches, can be used to carry excess water to the sides of the house and beyond the soil near the foundation (see illustration on page 23).

Property that falls away from a house at a rate of more than 1 vertical foot in 10 hor-

Retaining walls

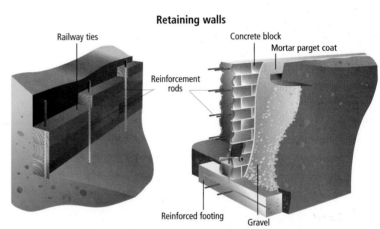

Railway ties   Concrete block   Mortar parget coat   Reinforcement rods   Reinforced footing   Gravel

SLOPE, RETAINING WALLS, AND BUILDING CODES

In many areas, building codes govern allowable slope and drainage near structures. These codes are expressed as formulas. When a slope drains toward a structure, the formula might read, "Footing to toe = H/2, but need not exceed 15 feet." This means that the distance from the base of the foundation—the footing—to the base of the slope—the toe—must equal at least the height (H) of the slope divided by 2. For example, the toe of a slope 10 feet high must not be closer than 5 feet to the foundation of a house to provide adequate room for drainage. The maximum distance for any slope is usually 15 feet. Employees in your local building department will help you understand local codes.

Building codes also cover the construction of retaining walls. A retaining wall usually must be set back from a property line 1 foot for every 1 foot of height. Retaining walls higher than 3 feet need to be designed by a structural engineer.

izontal feet requires grading and reshaping to be used for a patio. In some instances, it might be possible to move and rearrange soil to create a proper surface. If the slope is steep enough, you might have to construct one or more retaining walls to terrace the property (see illustrations on pages 24–25).

Whatever your ground slope, your finished patio project must provide some slope away from your house so that water does not collect near the foundation. A grade of about 2 vertical inches for every 8 horizontal feet provides enough slope for patio construction.

Shade

Shade changes throughout the day as the sun moves across the sky. The location of shade also changes over the course of a year. Decks and patios usually are placed in areas where afternoon shade is available during the hottest months—on the east side of houses or under large trees. Having a deck or patio that wraps around two or more sides of your house provides the flexibility of moving in and out of sunny or shaded areas.

If the configuration of your property does not allow you to use natural shade patterns, you might want to plan for shade structures that offer relief from the sun (see pages 64-69, "Built-ins & Privacy Screens," and pages 70-73, "Overheads"). Remember that shade structures do not necessarily provide shade directly underneath. Later in the day, when the sun begins to set but still provides heat, the shade provided by an arbor or pergola will be cast farther to the east. If you will use your outdoor patio or deck primarily in the evening hours, plan your shade structure with that in mind, or consider adding a vertical shade screen that blocks low-angled summer sunlight.

Below: Shade greatly affects the comfort of a deck or patio, especially during the warmest part of the summer. This illustration shows shade patterns at 5 p.m. in mid-July, just as the evening shade is beginning to overtake the patio.
Right: An overhead shade structure—in this case an arbor with 2×6s set on edge—helps cast shadows later in the day.

Views

If you have great views, orient your deck or patio project to take advantage of them, even compromising certain design principles if necessary to enjoy your views. For instance, you might be willing to expose your deck or patio to harsh western sun to be able to watch sunsets over the ocean. Or you might decide to build an expensive two-story deck on a steep lot so that you can face mountain vistas.

As you make planning sketches, show the direction of the views from your property. In some instances, the best views are obscured by trees. If views are important, consider selectively cutting trees to create interesting lines of sight.

If you are unsure about taking down trees, consult a landscape architect or designer so you won't destroy rare or important members of your landscape.

Above: An expansive porch affords views of a distant lake in beautiful British Columbia.

Planning with a Purpose

Establishing clear goals is the key to success.

Make sure your deck or patio fulfills your expectations with careful planning. Thorough planning means setting clear goals, establishing a budget, being familiar with the construction process, and making informed decisions that keep the project running smoothly.

Planning proceeds in stages. Set primary goals by determining how you'll use the space and how elaborate the finished space will be. The more precise your goals, the more satisfactory the results. For example, increasing your outdoor living space is a good objective, but if you specifically envision quiet get-togethers for two or three close friends, you might be happy with an intimate deck or patio that features room for a table and a few chairs. If you prefer expansive parties for twenty or more, plan a deck or patio large enough for two or three good-size tables and even outdoor cooking and clean-up areas.

Make sure your project is architecturally compatible with the exterior of your home and the surrounding landscape. Consider hiring a professional such as an architect, landscape architect, or designer. A professional will help express your ideas on paper and will ensure the project is structurally sound and meets local codes, covenants, and setback distances. A qualified architect or designer can help reduce overall costs by anticipating problems and offering creative solutions before work begins.

Creating little areas with distinct personalities makes this small backyard patio seem larger. The straight-line brick paths and the curved flagstone walls provide visual variety while a mix of shade-loving plants unifies the overall scheme. The stone wall that provides additional seating spirals into a small water feature only 18 inches in diameter. Who says a pond has to be large?

Creating different levels and areas gives your design flexibility. For a small group, you can confine your activities to one portion or level of your deck or patio. If larger gatherings are expected, you can expand to other areas. You don't need to have a large deck or patio to achieve a flexible design. Use planters, furnishings, or overhead structures such as pergolas or arbors to create and define components of your overall living area.

As you plan, keep in mind which conveniences would be appropriate. Including several electrical outlets, for example, makes it easy to add or move pole and table lamps, hook up a portable stereo, or plug in a laptop computer.

Getting ideas on paper

Begin planning by making sketches. The sketches record your thoughts, work out the scale and proportion of various design ideas, and visualize details. The most important reason to make sketches is to communicate your ideas to architects, builders, and other professionals who are part of your project team.

There is no need to make perfect drawings. It's important to use sketches as a way to make sure all design considerations—such as traffic patterns and the location of significant landscape features—are integrated into the final plan. Keep all of your sketches on file so you can see how your design ideas evolved.

Sketches showing a view from above are *plan views* (below). Sketches showing views from the side or front are *elevations*. Plan views account for the arrangement of space, clearances between furnishings, traffic patterns, and the relationship of a deck or patio to the surrounding yard and environment. Elevations give a sense of scale and help refine the design of vertical elements such as railings and privacy fences.

Below: Shade plays an all-important role in determining the location of outdoor living areas. Patterns of shade in late afternoon and evening are especially important because that's usually when it's time to relax or entertain. A plan view shows the arrangement of a property's key elements (left) and patterns of shade in late afternoon (right).

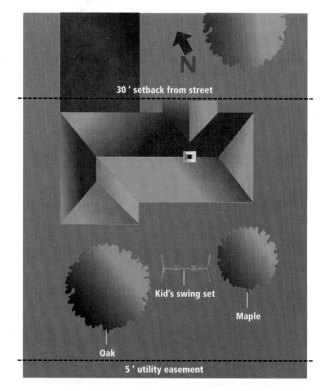

N

30 ' setback from street

Kid's swing set

Maple

Oak

5 ' utility easement

Shade at 6 p.m., June - Aug.

A good place to start making sketches is with a plat of your property (see page 22, "Your property's shape"). A plat is a plan view that shows the size and shape of your lot. Setbacks and easements also are shown.

Copy your plat onto graph paper. Indicate the position and footprint of your house and any ancillary structures, such as a garage or shed. Indicate which direction is north, and sketch in any major landscaping features, such as trees or a garden area. For trees, draw in the approximate trunk diameter, then lightly indicate the outer edges of the foliage. With trees placed, add the shade patterns for the time of day you are most likely to use your deck. At this point, you might want to make photocopies of this basic map. If you change your plans or want to compare different ideas, you can easily start fresh with a new basic map.

Incorporating landscaping

Decks and patios are transitional spaces that blend indoor rooms with outside environments. Significant landscaping features, such as trees and existing gardens, should be carefully integrated into your plans. When planning, remember these key points:
■ Trees are major features of well-planned outdoor rooms. They provide shade, privacy, and natural focal points. Make every effort to incorporate existing trees into your design. You can add trees, but the cost of installing a tree large enough to provide shade—one with a trunk that is 3 to 6 inches in diameter—can be $500 to $1,000.

Large trees might be right in the middle of your proposed deck or patio area. With a little ingenuity, you can build around them. Having a large shade tree growing through the middle of a deck creates a delightful

COMPUTER-AIDED DESIGN
Computer-based design programs for landscaping are especially useful and have a variety of ready-made symbols and graphic images of plants and small structures that are easily placed and edited. Quality landscape-design programs are available at computer and electronics stores for $35 to $75.

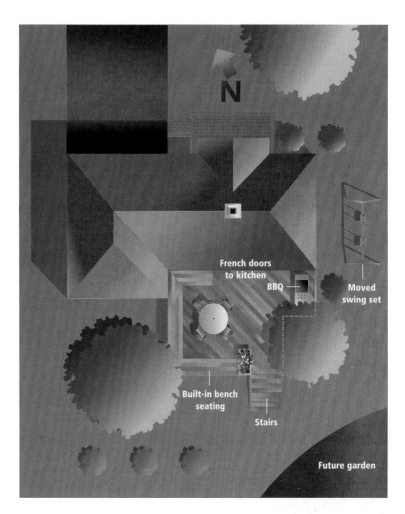

natural overhead shade structure for your new outdoor space.
■ Fast-growing vines are another way to provide shade and privacy. To take advantage of a vine, you'll need to plan a trellis for the vines to climb and you'll want the trellis structure to be integral to the overall design of your deck or patio. In the right conditions, a vine will grow 15 to 20 feet in a single season and provide plenty of leafy greenery by midsummer. Fast-climbing, flowering vines, such as trumpet vines and clematis, offer shade and sprays of beautiful flowers throughout the warmest months.
■ Foundation plantings can be important additions to your project, especially if you have a raised deck. Sturdy foundation plantings grow 2 to 4 feet high and help disguise footings, posts, and other structural components that might otherwise be exposed to view. When choosing foundation plantings, consider the amount of sunlight that will be

Above: Based on the patterns of shade illustrated by the diagrams (opposite page), this new deck is placed where it will receive evening shade from a backyard oak tree. The deck is angled to fit around a nearby maple. The design moves a swing set into a side yard that also receives evening shade.

Above: A large tree didn't deter plans for this backyard patio—the homeowners simply designed around it, making it a key element of design. The low stone wall around the tree doubles as seating. The flagstone floor is set in sand over landscaping fabric that inhibits weeds but lets moisture reach the tree's roots.

available for your plants after the project is complete. Certain portions of your deck or patio might be in full shade for most of the day, and you'll want to make sure to select appropriate plants.

■ To protect existing plants during construction, tell your building contractor to use every caution when installing footings for a deck or restructuring a sloped yard with retaining walls. A plant's root structure can be damaged during digging or by the pressure of heavy equipment moving over the ground. To prevent injury to trees, experts recommend building no closer than the tree's drip line—the outer edge of its foliage. Digging a few holes for foundation footings usually won't destroy a mature tree. Reduce possible root damage by designing a minimum of footings or using cantilevers that project your deck toward valuable trees and shrubs without using footings. To build a code-compliant cantilever, consult an architect or registered structural engineer.

Moving a favorite tree out of the way is an option. For $100 to $200, existing trees up to 6 inches in diameter can be transplanted by a tree service that has a truck-mounted tree spade. Look in the Yellow Pages of your telephone directory under "Tree Service" and "Landscape Contractors." For more information specific to your locality and type of tree, contact an arborist at your state university's agricultural department, or call your state's department of agriculture or county extension service—if they have the time, they'll provide free advice.

For a fee, you can contract the services of a design professional who specializes in landscaping (see "Working with a design professional" on page 35). A professional will make a map of your property, integrate your project ideas, and produce a plan that is as extensive as you'd like. Some landscape contractors combine design and installation services, although they might lack professional certification. Expect to pay $2,000 to

FURNISHING TYPE	MINIMUM SQUARE FOOTAGE REQUIRED	IDEAL SQUARE FOOTAGE FOR COMFORT
36" ROUND TABLE AND FOUR CHAIRS	A square or circle 9' across, a total of 80–90 square feet	A square or circle 12' across, a total of 140–150 square feet
48" ROUND TABLE AND SIX CHAIRS	A square or circle 10' across, a total of 100–110 square feet	A square or circle 13' across, a total of 160–180 square feet
ADIRONDACK CHAIR	A rectangle 6' long and 3.5' wide, a total of 21 square feet	A rectangle 8' long and 4' wide, a total of 32 square feet
BARBECUE GRILL, 18" DIAMETER KETTLE TYPE	1' clearance at sides and back, 3' clearance in front, a total of 20 square feet	2' clearance at sides and back, 4' clearance in front, a total of 42 square feet
BARBECUE GRILL ON 2'×3' ROLLING CART	1' clearance at sides and back, 3' clearance in front, a total of 30 square feet	2' clearance at sides and back, 4' clearance in front, a total of 56 square feet
FREESTANDING HAMMOCK WITH SELF-SUPPORTING STAND	A rectangle 9' long and 6' wide, a total of 54 square feet	A rectangle 9' x 6' , 3' at each side for clearance, a total of 108 square feet
BUILT-IN BENCH SEAT 6' LONG	6' wide, 1.5' wide seat, 3' clearance in front of seat, a total of 27 square feet	5' clearance in front of seat, a total of 39 square feet

$6,000 for a plan and installation of land-scaping features for an average-sized suburban house that include new borders, plantings, a 10×16 brick patio, and paths.

Harmonizing elements

It's important to establish visual harmony between your new deck or patio and the existing house. Compatibility should include the size and shape of the house, the types of materials used, and the scale and placement of stairs, railings, arbors, screens, and other elements. The best designs integrate key features with the size of the yard and existing plantings.

Although each piece of property is unique, creating harmony follows several commonsense rules of good design:

■ Take cues from the existing house. You don't have to reproduce elements precisely,

A simple brick patio is perfectly sized to accommodate a 48-inch round table and seating for six. More chairs under the pergola provide flexibility for entertaining larger gatherings.

but structural elements such as posts and railings should be thoughtfully selected and blend well with the overall design of the house. A low platform deck, for example, fits well with the shape and scale of a single-story ranch-style home. However, such a simple deck design would be out of place attached to a larger, ornate Victorian house. For that, you'd probably want to add posts and railings that complement decorative details from cornices or window trim, and possibly paint new elements to match existing woodwork.

■ Don't introduce new materials that are radically different from what already exists. A two-story brick home suggests using brick pavers for a patio, rather than elaborate stonework or plain concrete. When you mix textures and colors, be sure to add elements of the original. That plain concrete patio at the back of the two-story brick home will look a lot better if the concrete is tinted or stained to match the brick, or if it is surrounded by a border made of brick.

■ Scale is important. Don't get carried away and design a deck or patio that threatens to overwhelm the original house. Even if money is no object and you imagine the grandest of deck/patio combinations, the final design should be carefully scaled so that it is in proportion to the main house. Sketching different possibilities on paper helps you to visualize changes and to experiment with proportions. Even if you plan to hire a design professional, your own sketches are also a good way to start a productive dialogue about your preferences.

Connecting to inside rooms

It's exciting to imagine the ways your new deck or patio will change your outdoor environment, but it's just as important to remember how your project will change the use of adjacent interior spaces. New doorway locations and altered traffic patterns are a few of the possible consequences. If your new deck or patio is part of a more

Generous French doors let this airy, four-season entry room open directly to the backyard patio. Furnished with comfortable, casual chairs and featuring exterior walls with lots of windows, the entry room makes an easy transition to the outdoor spaces.

expansive renovation plan, make sure the traffic flows easily from one space to the other, and that the changes meet your goals for comfort and livability.

Kitchens and family rooms are good transition points for accessing a deck or patio. These areas usually are less formal and are natural places for kids and pets to wander in and out of the house. Wear-resistant vinyl or tile flooring stand up to traffic well and are easy to clean.

Having a door leading from a kitchen to a deck or patio provides easy access when entertaining. If you have a standard exterior door in this location, consider changing it to a sliding patio or a double French doorway

Working with a design professional

A professional designer creates a space that meets your needs. Because of their expertise and experience, professionals can offer fresh ideas, anticipate code restrictions, and deal with unusual problems. If the cost of hiring a designer seems prohibitive, consider that professionals can help save on overall costs by contributing to the efficiency of the project, by organizing and managing work flow, and by helping to avoid expensive mistakes. Many of them are willing to work as consultants for an hourly fee.

When working with a professional, good communication is key to achieving your goals. Start a clipping folder. Use it to keep articles and photographs cut from magazines that show ideas and design elements that appeal to you. Add product brochures or advertisements that you can show to your designer. Draw sketches of your ideas, and share them with your designer. A good designer is interested in your lifestyle and should ask questions and take notes about how you live, your daily routine, and your project goals.

Three types of design professionals can work on a deck or patio project. Although they have specialized areas of expertise, most professionals are well-versed in all phases of design and can help create a comprehensive plan.

■ *Architects* work primarily with structure and reorganization of space. They are familiar with many types of building materials, finishes, and structural systems. An architect is a good choice for complex deck designs. An architect will design your deck and make sure it is sensibly integrated with adjacent living areas, such as your kitchen or family room. Architects charge a percentage of the project's total cost, usually 10 to 15 percent. If hired on an hourly basis, they charge $50 to $125 per hour. For a listing of architects in your area, look in the Yellow Pages of your phone directory, or try the internet search engine offered by the American

for a larger opening and to expose interior rooms to views and light. Plan on spending $2,000 to $3,000 for a contractor to install a 6-foot-wide, sliding patio door, including all materials.

As you plan, sketch in traffic patterns from access doorways to deck or patio stairs and paths. These traffic patterns should be sensible and practical. Keep tables and eating areas well away from traffic. If possible, place grills and cooking equipment in out-of-the-way locations or in special niches built just for them. Leave plenty of legroom in front of built-in benches so that guests won't have to retract their legs every time someone walks past.

Above: A second-story deck is set amid the treetops and stays shady almost all day. The tree trunk fits through a cutout in the deck floor.

Institute of Architects at www.e-architect.com/reference/home.asp

■ *Landscape architects* registered with the American Society of Landscape Architects (ASLA) are usually designers only; the plans they furnish must be given to a landscape contractor for final installation. Occasionally, a professional landscape architect joins with a landscape contractor to offer full-service planning and installation. An ASLA architect will charge $75 to $125 per hour to inspect and analyze the property, and then complete detailed drawings that recommend plantings and landscape features which help connect the new space to the outdoor environment. To create a plan, expect to pay 15 percent of the cost of the finished landscape project. To find a landscape architect, consult the Yellow Pages of your telephone directory under "Landscape Architects," or check with the American Society of Landscape Architects at 202/898-2444 or www.asla.org.

■ *Landscape contractors* can install decks, patios, walkways, retaining walls, plantings, and ancillary structures such as pergolas and arbors. Many landscape contractors are full-service business firms that have landscape architects, designers, and installers, and can provide a full range of services that

include initial concepts, finalized plans, installation, and ongoing maintenance. If required by state law, a landscape contracting company should be licensed or certified, indicating they have passed examinations and have demonstrated expertise and knowledge, and that they participate in ongoing programs of education. Find "Landscape Contractors" in the Yellow Pages of your telephone directory or contact the Associated Landscape Contractors of America at 800/395-2522 or www.alca.org.

Adding electrical power

Careful planning of your electrical needs helps ensure your satisfaction when the project is complete. If you plan to use your new porch or sunroom as a supplemental kitchen, you might need individual circuits to run small appliances such as cooktops and rotisseries. A few electrical outlets ensures you'll

be able to plug in stereo equipment, supplemental lamps, or a laptop computer. Calculate your home's existing power requirements to determine if you'll need additional circuits to handle the increased load. A licensed electrical contractor can make these calculations and ensure your project conforms to the specifications set forth by the National Electrical Code (NEC®). A modest deck or patio usually can be serviced by splicing into an existing circuit. More extensive remodeling could require adding a circuit. Your design professional or general contractor should be able to provide a cost estimate for electrical work. If you are acting as your own general contractor, take bids from several electrical contractors to establish a price for the work.

Splicing into an existing circuit requires an electrician to locate an existing junction box to add wiring, or else add a junction box

at some point along a length of existing wiring. Junction boxes often are located in open attic or basement spaces where they are readily accessible. Occasionally, an electrician must open up walls and ceilings to access wiring and add new junction boxes—work that requires minor demolition. The cost of repairing walls and ceilings will be part of the cost of the project.

Outdoor receptacles should be placed in weatherproof boxes with spring-loaded outlet covers that seal against moisture. Also, most building codes require that outdoor receptacles be protected by a ground-fault circuit interrupter (GFCI). If there is a short circuit, GFCI-type receptacles detect the deviation in current and instantly shut off power to the receptacle.

Outdoor lighting

A well-designed outdoor lighting system allows you to use your deck or patio in comfort and safety during the evening. It should illuminate key points, such as conversation areas, cooking centers, doors, walkways, pool surrounds, and stairs. It also can be used to highlight special features, such as plants or trees, and can provide security lighting around foundation plantings and fences.

Outdoor lighting comes in three types: regular fixtures that use 120-volt household current, low-voltage, and solar-powered. Low-voltage lighting is increasingly popular because it is safe, inexpensive, and easy to install. Manufacturers of low-voltage lighting offer an array of styles and configurations made especially for outdoor residential use that are readily available at home improvement centers. Both the low-

Left: Small, low-voltage lights on slender rods spaced about 4 feet apart offer minimal illumination. But they enhance safety by helping to define key landscaping features such as the perimeter of the pond wall and the edges of flower beds. Low-voltage and solar-powered lights are easy for a homeowner to install.

Above: The experienced hand of a landscape architect is evident in this complex arrangement of outdoor spaces that includes flagstone steps, a patio, a curved swimming pool, plantings, and a gazebo that resembles a tropical hut.

voltage and solar lights are either freestanding units or fasten to posts, railings, stair risers, and other components.

Lamps, or bulbs, cast different kinds of light. The familiar incandescent bulbs are relatively inexpensive. They have a warm, natural quality of light that is especially pleasing on faces. These lights can be dimmed with rheostat switches—a real advantage for design flexibility. Quartz-type incandescent lamps provide a more intense "whiter" light.

High-intensity discharge (HID) lamps include metal halide, mercury vapor, and high-pressure sodium lamps. All provide reliable, brilliant light and are especially energy-efficient, but they are not recommended for use with dimmer switches. Some people are bothered by the orange or greenish cast of the light from HID lamps. They are used primarily for safety lighting around pools, or for illuminating large activity areas, such as tennis courts.

When planning a lighting scheme, keep the design as flexible as possible so that your lighting is appropriate for a variety of uses. Use several circuits, and plan for dimmer switches that allow you to control the amount of light in individual areas. Place switches indoors.

If you also want switches outdoors, you'll need to have 3-way switches installed. To avoid annoying glare, make sure the light source—the bulb—is hidden from direct view by using shades, covers, or plantings, or by letting light bounce off large reflective surfaces such as walls.

An outdoor lighting system usually is a combination of several lighting techniques. The most common types are:

■ *Downlighting* is placed on poles, in trees, or on the sides of houses. It shines directly onto surfaces and is used for general illumination and safety.

■ *Uplighting* is placed low to the ground and directed upward. It is used for dramatic effect and to highlight individual objects such as unusual trees or garden sculptures.

■ *Passage lighting* illuminates pathways and

stairs. A series of small downlights usually are used to lead the way along a defined route.

■ *Area lighting* illuminates larger surfaces such as lawns, patios, and decks. Area lighting usually uses several types of lighting to produce an overall effect that is not too harsh or distracting.

Setting budget priorities

A workable budget usually is a compromise between all the great things you imagine for your finished project and what you ought to budget to achieve your goals. Your first priority should be to set limits for the total amount of money you'll spend. As a guide, make two lists. One list should include everything you consider essential for your new space. The other list should be the extras—the amenities you'd like to have if there's money left over after you pay for essentials. Don't add extras until costs for the essentials are finalized.

As you complete your ideas and move toward construction, you'll need to get bids from contractors and other professionals. Add a 5- to 10-percent "cushion" to the total figure to cover cost overruns and changes to plans that can occur after construction has begun. Have a firm idea of what you'd like to spend and tell it to all of the professionals involved in your project. A commitment to your bottom line will help you make the difficult cost-cutting decisions if your project threatens to go over budget.

Below: An imaginative railing system—featuring built-in flower boxes with solid and lattice panels stained forest green—is right at home in this woodsy setting.

All Decked Out

Learning about the materials and methods of deck construction is the first important step in building the deck of your dreams.

A well-planned deck should be a natural extension of your house, complementing the form, color, and details of the main structure. To make sure your deck looks great and fits your lifestyle, take the time to learn basic construction terms and the kinds of materials best suited for building decks. With that knowledge, you'll be able to make informed decisions that will allow your deck project to proceed smoothly and efficiently.

Not too many years ago, most decks were built with basic construction techniques and inexpensive materials—usually green pressure-treated wood. The results were sturdy, serviceable decks that had little in common with the house. Today's homeowner has an enormous array of deck materials, finishes, and embellishments from which to select. There also are many publications that have photographs of imaginative shapes and configurations, each presenting inspiring ideas and ingenious solutions. As you plan, learn about as many of the possibilities as you can. The result will be a deck that enhances the value of your property and is a joy to use.

When the owners of this Illinois house, built in 1945, decided they needed more living space, a deck was high on their list. Instead of hiring a contractor, the family did the work themselves, studying deck construction and purchasing materials from a local home improvement center.

Styles

Many factors will have an impact on the design of your deck. These can include the architectural style of your house, contours of your property, restrictions imposed by setbacks and codes, and location of major landscaping features, such as large trees and outbuildings. In basic terms, a single-level, ranch-style house would probably look best with a low, platform-style deck. Such a simple deck would probably look out of place on a larger, more elaborate home. There, a multilevel deck with interesting overheads—such as a pergola or arbor—would help keep the design in proportion.

Deck designs are so diverse that it's difficult to pinpoint a particular style. However, identifying the five basic configurations is a good place to begin the design of your deck.

■ *Platform decks* are the simplest form of deck. They are usually built on level lots and are attached to single-level dwellings. The platform deck is so low to the ground that railings often aren't necessary. Most building codes require railings and balusters if the deck is 24 inches or more from the ground—be sure to check your local building codes before proceeding.

On gently sloped lots, you can build a series of platform decks that step down gradually to follow the contour of the land. Even though railings might not be required, you can give substance and mass to platform decks by including built-in planters and bench seating around the perimeter.

Because platform decks are close to the ground, it is especially important for the

Below: A platform deck is built low to the ground. If the decking surface is not more than 24 inches from the ground, railings usually aren't required. However, built-in bench seating or planters help define the deck perimeter.

materials used to be impervious to moisture. Structural materials for any deck should be pressure treated or rated for direct contact with the ground. For decking and other platform deck parts, make sure all materials receive two coats of protective sealer before they are installed so that undersides are well-preserved. In humid areas, install a vapor barrier of plastic sheeting before construction begins. Cover the vapor barrier with 2 or 3 inches of soil or a layer of gravel to conceal it from view.

■ *Raised decks* are common because most houses sit on foundation walls that position the first-level floor several feet above grade. Raised decks require railing systems for safety and stairs to make the deck accessible to the yard. Designing good-looking railing systems and locating stairs so that they establish practical traffic patterns are keys to successful deck planning.

Raised decks have foundation posts that are exposed to view when the structure is complete. The structural members can be concealed with foundation plantings—such

as shrubs—or with skirting. Skirting usually consists of lath or lattice panels that are cut to fit between the deck surface and the ground. The cut paneling is attached to perimeter posts. This type of skirting hides the structural system yet permits air to circulate underneath the deck, discouraging problems such as rot or mold that are associated with excessive moisture. Lattice panels also prevent certain large animals, such as raccoons or skunks, from taking a liking to the protected area under your deck. For more information on skirting, see page 62.

■ *Two-story decks* provide outdoor access to upper-level areas of your home. The structural posts and bracing required to support a two-story deck can be quite tall and present an aesthetic challenge. Posts can be made thicker than codes require or they can be faced with decorative boards so they won't appear spindly. Partial skirting or decorative pieces spanning exterior posts help create a balanced design.

■ *Multilevel decks* are a series of decks connected by stairways or walkways. They are

Above: Many newer houses include decks as a standard feature of the construction. The raised deck on this custom-built house has access to three different rooms through large glass doors.

Below: Second-level decks must take into account the appearance of the exposed structural members. This example uses decorative lattice arches between support posts to incorporate the posts into the overall design. Opposite: Freestanding decks often feature whimsical designs.

usually designed for yards with sloped lots so that the deck areas follow the contours of the land. A tall main deck that otherwise might gain access to the surrounding yard through a long stairway can be built as a series of smaller, unique deck spaces, each joined by a short run of stairs. This arrangement prevents the lowest deck—the one farthest from the house—from interfering with views from decks higher up.

Use a multilevel deck to take advantage of microclimates within your yard. Have one

level close to the house for entertaining, another one in the cool shade of nearby trees, and yet another placed to take in the sun.

■ *Freestanding decks* are not attached to the house. These separate landscaping features usually are located some distance from the main living areas where they can provide the best views or be positioned in a shady glade or in a beautiful garden. Freestanding decks are built with the same methods and techniques as attached decks.

Components

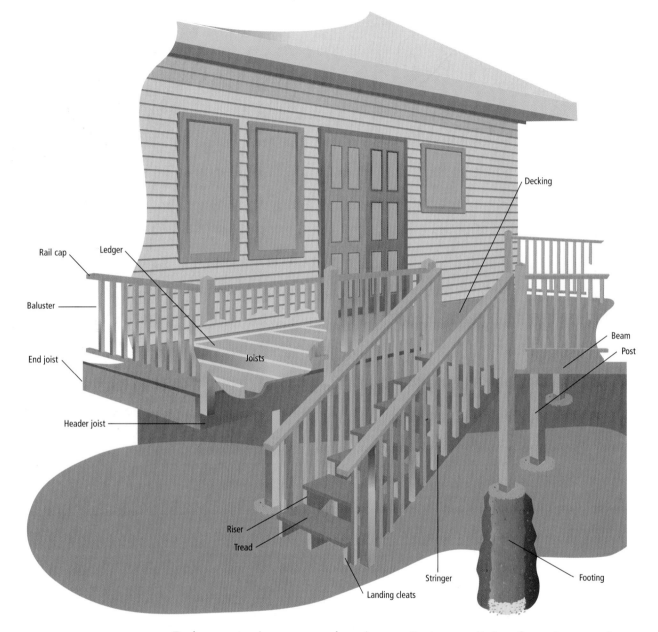

Rail cap

Ledger

Baluster

End joist

Header joist

Joists

Decking

Beam

Post

Riser

Tread

Landing cleats

Stringer

Footing

Decks are simple structures, but the final design can be complex. Becoming familiar with the terms used in deck construction is essential when planning a deck, ordering materials, and overseeing any changes to plans while the deck is being built. An understanding of deck terminology will help you communicate effectively with designers, builders, and other contractors. Here are some important terms:

■ *Footings* are cylinders of poured concrete that extend into the ground and support individual posts. Building codes require that they must extend below the frost line. This prevents the seasonal cycles of freezing and thawing from disturbing the position of the footings over the years. A footing usually will be 36 to 42 inches deep. The location of the footings depends on the size and shape of the deck.

■ *Pier blocks* are made of precast concrete and

are about 8 inches on each side. Precast pier blocks are set on top of footings while the footing concrete is still wet. They elevate the posts to keep them from coming into contact with the ground, preventing moisture damage. Some pier blocks include metal hardware for a secure connection to posts.

■ *Posts* extend up from the footings and form the vertical supports of a deck. The thickness of the posts depends on the configuration of the deck structure. Thicker posts spaced farther apart can take the place of thinner posts that are closer together. Posts should be made of pressure-treated lumber to retard rot and insect attack. Tall posts—such as those required for second-story decks—need angled supports called bracing to provide stability.

■ *Joists* form a grid for supporting the decking material. Often called "two-by" lumber, joists are 1½ inches thick, and are installed on edge. The sizes of the joists are determined by the span of the deck; the longer the span, the heftier the joist. The joists at the perimeter of a deck are called "rim joists." Rim joists usually are doubled to provide firm support around the deck edges.

■ *Girders* are large pieces of lumber used to support joists. The girders are attached to the posts and run at right angles to the joists. Depending on the size and configuration of a deck, girders may not be necessary. Like all structural components, girders made from pressure-treated lumber combine strength and durability.

■ *Ledger board* is a joist mounted against the side of a house to provide support for one side of a deck. The ledger is bolted or screwed to the house and the space behind the ledger is sealed with caulk and covered with flashing to prevent water from penetrating to the interior of the house. Joists usually are attached to the ledger with joist

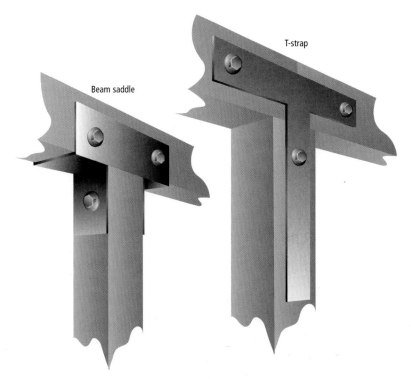

Beam saddle

T-strap

hangers—galvanized metal holders that provide firm, secure support.

■ *Fascia boards* are used to cover rim joists. They are usually 1-inch-thick boards made from a good-looking wood such as cedar or redwood and often are used to cover joists made from pressure-treated lumber. For a clean, finished appearance, fascia may be mitered at the corners. Wood exposed to harsh, outdoor climates is bound to expand and contract, opening even the tightest miter joists over time.

■ *Decking* covers joists and forms the main surface area of a deck. Decking is usually installed flat and is fastened with galvanized nails or screws. Decking boards are spaced ⅛ to ³⁄₁₆ inches apart to provide drainage and to allow for the natural contraction and expansion of the wood (see pages 48–53 for more information about decking).

Above: Galvanized metal hardware fastens pieces of lumber together and makes an exceptionally strong, stable connection. Metal connectors come in many sizes and shapes for a variety of applications.

Decking

Most of your deck is a large, flat surface—decking. Because decking is such a prominent feature, it should be attractive, durable, smooth, and free of cracks, splinters, and other defects.

Wooden decking is easy to work with and comes in a range of prices to fit any budget. Today's marketplace also offers a number of synthetic products that resemble wood. These products usually are more expensive than wood, but most are virtually maintenance-free. Because decks are so popular, different types of decking materials are widely available in all areas.

Wood decking

Several types of wood are used for decking, railing systems, and embellishments such as planters, pergolas, and built-in furniture. These woods have attractive grain patterns and colors. Almost all wood turns silvery gray when exposed to the elements. To preserve the original color of wood such as cedar and redwood, you should clean it and apply clear sealer every year. Popular deck materials include:

■ *Redwood* is naturally resistant to rot and decay. It should be treated with clear sealers each year. It is a soft wood with a distinctive reddish hue and has a tight, uniform grain pattern that is exceptionally attractive. It is also an excellent paint-grade wood, although

Right: For greater visual impact, install your decking in an interesting pattern. Decking installed in a basket-weave dresses up this otherwise plain platform deck.

Left: Long, narrow decks look best with decking installed parallel to the face of the house. This standard pattern features cedar decking fastened perpendicular to joists. Keeping the warm brown tones of the wood requires regular cleaning and applying a sealer at least once a year.

the cost of redwood would suggest it should be used in its natural state for best effect.

■ *Cedar* is lightweight and naturally resistant to rot and decay. It has streaks of cream and brown and has occasional knots. The 1×6 cedar boards made specifically as decking material are 5½ inches wide, a full 1 inch thick, and have rounded edges that prevent splintering. Cedar decking is widely available.

■ *Cypress* also is lightweight and naturally resistant to rot and decay. It is a soft wood with a varied grain pattern and is mostly available in the South.

■ *Pressure-treated wood* is widely used as decking. It is strong and costs less than other decking materials. It comes in green or brown, the result of chemicals that resist moisture, decay, and attack from insects. Some people think the color is unattractive; however, pressure-treated wood can be stained or painted. Pressure-

treated wood combines great strength with low cost, and it's available throughout North America.

Construction lumber often is used for the structural parts of a deck—the posts, girders, and joists. When exposed to the elements, the surface of the medium-grade fir or pine used for structural parts tends to crack and split, although it doesn't lose its strength. Because these components are usually hidden from view, the appearance of the material is not a concern.

Construction-grade, pressure-treated wood should not be used for decking. Instead, be sure to specify pressure-treated 1×6s that are manufactured especially for use as decking. This material is 5½ inches wide, a full 1 inch thick (also referred to as ⁵⁄₄ thickness), has few knots, and has rounded edges that resist splintering.

MATERIAL	COLOR	STRENGTH	AVAILABILITY	COST — 1 LINEAL FOOT OF 1×6
REDWOOD	Pink to deep red; might have streaks of cream-colored sapwood	Low to moderate strength	Usually available in most areas of the country	$1.50
CEDAR	Light tan to medium brown with streaks of cream	Low	Readily available in most areas of the country	$0.85
CYPRESS	Various browns	Low	Available mostly in the South	$0.65
PRESSURE-TREATED PINE OR FIR	Tinted green or brown	Medium	Widely available	$0.45
IPE	Lustrous chocolate brown	High	Available only by special order	$3.50 to $4
SYNTHETICS: RUBBER, VINYL, PLASTIC, AND COMPOSITES	Pure white, tan, gray, and various browns	Used only for decking, not any structural components	Usually available, but not all products may be available at one location	$2 to $4

Diagonal

Chevron

Basket weave

Double diagonal

Herringbone

Standard

Decking patterns can be an important design element. Each pattern must have a particular joist layout so that the ends of the decking boards are adequately supported.

■ *Ipe* is a tropical hardwood that is increasingly popular for deck construction. It is heavy, expensive, and difficult to cut and drill. However, it is impervious to the elements, resists insect attacks, and has the same fire rating as concrete or steel. Best of all, it's a beautiful, lustrous brown color. Order ipe from a hardwood dealer.

Synthetic decking

Several kinds of synthetic decking materials are available as alternatives to wood. Some have wood-like textures and can be cut and fastened with the same tools and techniques used for wood. However, most are not strong enough to be used as structural members and are intended only for decking. They cost more than wood of similar sizes, but, except for occasional cleaning, they are maintenance-free.

■ *Plastic decking* comes in several colors and textures. It is lightweight and easy to install with a special system of clips that allows the decking to expand and contract.

■ *Vinyl decking* has similar properties to plastic, and is available in a variety of colors. The nonslip textured surface resembles manufactured metal rather than wood. Look for brands that have ultraviolet (UV) light inhibitors impregnated into the material.

Left: Few decking materials are as beautiful as redwood. With its rich color, tight grain, and natural resistance to decay, redwood has a reputation as one of the premier woods for exterior use. Redwood is increasingly rare and expensive. Cedar makes an attractive alternative and has many of the same characteristics.

Above: Synthetic decking, such as this composite material, is maintenance-free and won't splinter or crack, even in the harshest conditions. Composites usually are made with recycled plastics.

UV inhibitors prevent fading due to exposure to sunlight.

■ *Composite lumber* is made from wood fibers mixed with resins derived from recycled plastic. This decking is the most realistic-looking of the synthetics, is easy to cut and nail, and can be stained.

■ *Rubber lumber* is made from a mixture of recycled plastics and recycled rubber from old tires. It comes in only a few colors, but it is tough, durable, and impervious to rot, insect attack, and UV light.

Decking patterns

Decking usually is installed in long strips run parallel to the face of the house and perpendicular to joists. You can add visual interest by installing decking diagonally, or by making patterns that display creative flair. Patterned decking is one way to break up the expanse of a large deck.

Patterns should be planned to avoid partial grids or incomplete patterns at the deck's perimeter. Some patterns require additional joists or structural framing to provide enough nailing surfaces for the ends of the decking boards. You can create interesting decking patterns only by drawing plans that show the proper framing. For illustrations of some popular patterns, see page 50.

■ *Standard patterns* have the decking running perpendicular to the joists and parallel to the longest face of the house. This is the least expensive and least complicated way to install decking.

■ *Diagonal decking* usually is installed with the decking at 45 degrees to the joists. Altering the joist pattern or adding joists usually is not necessary, but angled cuts at the ends of the decking wastes more wood and requires 5 to 10 percent more boards than a standard pattern.

■ *Parquet or grid patterns* are modular squares featuring decking boards that change directions. A common practice is to have the boards of each square run perpendicular to the adjacent squares. A variation is a geometric pattern of modular grids featuring diagonal decking.

Left: Durable and attractive, cedar is a natural choice for this rustic cottage set in a wooded area. The diagonal decking pattern adds visual interest.

Railings & Stairs

Railings and stairs often take center stage in a deck design. These important components are closely linked by function and are often the most prominent elements of a deck's appearance. Successful deck projects usually include imaginative designs for railings and stairs so the deck has personality and charm. Before you begin to design stairs and railings, become familiar with your local building codes so that construction complies with all requirements. Remember that it's difficult to design railings and stairs accurately, so that all posts and balusters are evenly spaced and all steps are of equal height. If you aren't sure of your design abilities, it's best to work with a professional.

Railings

To enhance safety, most building codes require railings on decks that are more than 24 inches above the ground. Railings also are key design elements. The most attractive railings harmonize with the style of the

Right: A classic Arts-and-Crafts-style railing with squared balusters and posts suits the style of this 60-year-old Minneapolis bungalow. Notice that every third baluster is slightly over-sized, adding visual texture to the design. Post tops house low-voltage outdoor lights behind translucent panels.

Left: This whimsical railing system is made entirely of maple branches. The posts were drilled out and set over steel rods imbedded in the concrete foundation walls. The gaps between branches conform to local codes, but consult with your building inspector before designing this type of system. Below: Horizontal runs of galvanized steel pipe form a striking yet inexpensive deck railing for this Des Moines home.

Right: Easy and inexpenisve to build, this classic deck railing features 6×6 posts, 2×4 rails, and square, 2×2 balusters. Trim around the post tops adds a touch of flair. Below: Two platform decks connected by low, broad steps create distinct areas for eating and for entertaining. The upper deck features an overhead sunscreen; the lower portion is open to the sky.

Left: A spiral staircase is a graceful and space-saving way to access a second-level deck from the ground. It's useful for tight quarters, such as this small backyard. The steel railing system of the staircase is echoed by a railing that has the same slender balusters.

house, echoing prominent details or enhancing certain style motifs. The railing on a deck attached to a classic older home, for example, might repeat fanciful trim from an eave or cornice. A railing on a deck attached to a contemporary home might be sleek and simple. A handsome, imaginative railing might not be much more expensive to build than a basic one, and it transforms your deck from an ordinary platform into a striking outdoor living area.

Railings include support posts. To keep railings strong, building codes limit the space between railing posts, usually to 4 to 6 feet. The posts along the perimeter of the deck can actually be a part of the deck's structural system. One end can rest on a footing, and the post can extend up past the decking to be part of the railing system. Joists and girders are attached to the post below the decking. This type of railing system is especially stable. Otherwise, posts are attached separately, usually by bolting the post to the outside of the rim joists.

Between the posts are horizontal members: the rails. A railing system is either made entirely of horizontal rails or can include vertical members called balusters.

Balusters come in a variety of shapes. The simplest are square; the most decorative are "turned" balusters that have delicate flutes, ridges, and grooves. These basic components can be arranged in many ways to form railings that can be anything from classic to experimental, as long as the final design meets building codes. Most codes require that the space between balusters or horizontal rails be no greater than 4 inches.

Railings usually are made of wood, although strong materials such as steel, copper tubing, and heavy-gauge wire also are used if your construction methods are approved by local building codes. Wood can be left natural, stained, or painted. Even with regular applications of clear weather sealers, natural wood eventually will turn a soft, silvery gray. Stained wood shows its grain pattern and is relatively easy to maintain because preparing the surface with scraping and sanding isn't necessary. Painted

wood railings are dramatic and are easy to match or contrast with the color of your house. To minimize repainting, use only top-quality exterior paints; applying fresh coats of paint between balusters requires a steady hand and lots of patience.

Stairs

A well-designed stairway is expressive, inviting, and safe. Stairs provide a natural, easy transition between your home's interior and your yard. The design should channel traffic away from living spaces and obstructions. Plan a walking corridor 3 feet wide that leads from exterior doors to the stairs. Make sure that people using the corridor aren't forced to walk around seating areas, cooking stations, and structural members such as posts.

Stairs can take many forms, but all designs must conform to local building codes. Building codes usually specify the

Alternative railing materials

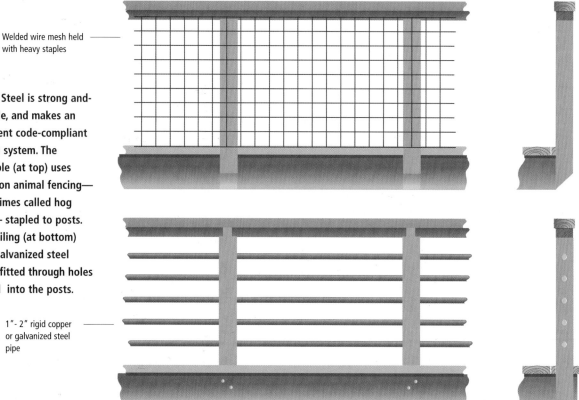

Welded wire mesh held with heavy staples

1"- 2" rigid copper or galvanized steel pipe

Above: White, painted railings give any deck a refined appearance, and they blend well with natural decking materials. This railing has a double top rail—a simple but stylish touch.

maximum rise of a step to be 7½ inches, and the minimum width of a tread to be 10 to 11 inches, for a total rise and run of 17 to 18 inches. Although stairs can't be steeper than specified, they usually can be lower, as long as the design is approved by your building codes. A 4-inch-high step, for example, needs a tread 13 to 14 inches wide. Platform steps are a series of shallow decks and work well on gentle slopes where they can hover above the contours of the land.

Stairs for elevated decks require careful consideration. The total run of the stairway can be quite long and might project awkwardly into your yard. To compensate, design stairs that make one or two turns and follow the outside edges of the deck. Stairs built this way can hide posts and other structural members. Stairways that change direction require landings—short platforms at least 3 feet by 3 feet. Larger landings can have built-in seating and planters, creating "interim" decks that complement the overall design of the structure.

Stairs for decks usually have "open" risers with no wood enclosing the vertical, rear part of each step. A system with open risers helps prevent water, leaves, and other debris from accumulating at the intersection of the tread and the riser. This kind of debris can lead to moisture damage and rot.

Posts and balusters attached directly
to perimeter rim joists

Rails installed on edge

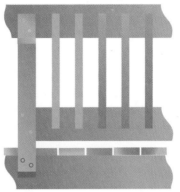

Balusters installed between horizontal rails;
railing cap runs over posts

Balusters installed between horizontal
rails; post tops extend above railing

1×4 boards used as balusters

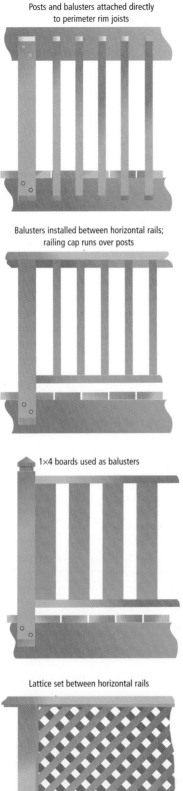

Code-compliant railing
systems take many forms
and can be made of a
variety of materials. The
key to strength and safety
is to have posts securely
bolted to a structural
member, such as a rim
joist, and to have spaces
no larger than 4 inches
between any of the
components. Have your
railing system plans
checked by your local
building department
before you commit
to building it.

Steel or copper tubing

Lattice set between horizontal rails

Skirting

Skirting is installed under the deck platform along the perimeter of the deck. Its primary function is to hide the structural system from view. It also keeps animals from wandering under your deck and perhaps even nesting there. Skirting usually is made of lath or panels of wood with decorative holes that permit air to circulate, discouraging moisture problems such as rot or mold. Elaborate skirting can be made of boards, solid panels, or masonry walls with vent holes to allow air circulation. Remember that skirting is not a required component. You might decide that your deck looks better without it.

Although the role of skirting is primarily functional, it's a prominent surface and should be considered a key element of deck design. Lath panels, for example, are "busy" components that compete for attention with stairs and railings. To camouflage skirting, stain or paint it a neutral background color, such as gray or dark brown. Bring in foundation plantings that will fill in around your

deck and cover at least part of the skirting.

Sketch ideas before committing to a final design. Because the lower edge of the skirting is close to the ground, it should be made from pressure-treated or rot-resistant wood, such as redwood or cedar. Untreated wood should be given several coats of a water sealer or preservative before installation.

If possible, install your skirting in individual sections that can be easily removed for maintenance, repair, or replacement. Include a hinged or easily removable section that will permit access to the area underneath the deck for inspections and repairs.

Above: This deck is skirted with an all-masonry foundation wall that supports structural members. Solid skirting walls must have ventilation holes to permit air circulation and prevent moisture problems. Right: With the exception of the stair treads and the decking, all components of this classic-style deck, including the skirting, are painted white to match the siding of the house. Foundation plantings help soften the look of the skirting.

Above: Lattice skirting helps hide the structural members of this Maryland deck. Low masonry planter boxes, in turn, help hide the skirting. Left: Staining this lattice skirting an earth-tone brown color helps blend it into the shadows underneath the deck.

Built-ins & Privacy Screens

Backrest

Seat support

Legs

Joists

Carriage bolts

Reinforcing plate

Built-in benches, planters, privacy screens, and cooking centers all are options that add comfort and convenience. Planning built-ins encourages you to get the most from your outdoor spaces by determining how you'll use your deck and how components will be arranged. Built-ins usually are constructed of the same materials as your deck and are cost-effective ways to provide seating, privacy, and staging areas for your favorite activities. Here are some common built-ins:

■ *Benches* provide permanent seating. The supporting members of the bench—the legs and backrest—usually are integral to construction of the deck. The legs and backrest are fastened with bolts directly to structural components such as joists or posts; decking material is cut to fit around them.

Bench seats should be 15 to 18 inches from the floor of the deck, and 15 inches deep. Benches built around the perimeter of a low deck can double as railings. However, if a deck is more than 24 inches from the ground, benches

must conform to the building codes that apply to railings. This means that the back of the bench should be 36 to 42 inches high to prevent accidents if someone stands on the bench seat. Added to the height of the seat, the total height of a back could be 60 inches from the floor of the deck. Be sure to check your local building codes to determine requirements for built-in benches. Built-in benches that are not used as railings can be built in any style.

■ *Planters* bring the natural beauty of greenery and flowering plants to deck design. They are permanent structures that should integrate with the overall style of the deck. On low decks, they help define the edges or perimeter of the deck and give substance to otherwise plain deck structures. Planters should not be used as a substitute for code-compliant railings.

Make planters from moisture-resistant woods such as cedar, redwood, cypress, or pressure-treated lumber. For annual or perennial flowers, make planters 8 to 12 inches deep. For shrubs, planters should be 18 to 24 inches deep. The bottom of the planters should have drainage holes that extend completely through the decking

Above: A screen doesn't have to be substantial to be effective. This simple screen is made of open lattice yet provides a comfortable feeling of enclosure and privacy.

material. Bore 1-inch holes every 12 inches throughout the floor of the planter.

To ensure that your planter has a long life and to prevent soils from leaching out and staining decking, line your planter with a waterproof membrane. Use plastic sheeting at least 3 millimeters thick or 15-pound roofing felt—sometimes called tar paper. Start at the bottom and wrap the membrane up the sides. Overlap edges at least 4 inches. Cut openings in the membrane over the drainage holes. An alternative to using plastic sheeting is to coat the interior walls of

the planter with roofing tar. Apply it carefully, though, because if gets on the wood it will stain.

Solid materials, such as fiberglass or galvanized steel, make the best liners. Make fiberglass liners out of flexible fiberglass cloth and paintable hardeners from a boat repair kit. A sheet metal shop can prepare custom-made galvanized steel liners to fit exactly inside a planter. It's important to select materials carefully; for example, galvanized steel should not be used with planters made of cedar. When both materials are wet

Left: Built-in planter boxes flank a short set of steps leading to this platform deck. Backless benches built around the perimeter define the edge of the deck. Because this deck is built low to the ground, the benches do not have to conform to railing heights specified by building codes. Below: Simple planter box construction uses decking that also was used as siding and a marine-grade plywood bottom with drainage holes. The liner is plastic sheeting.

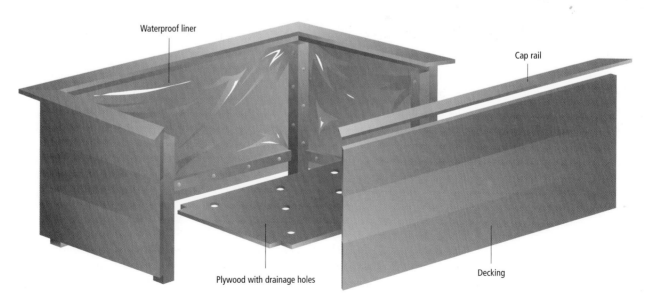

Waterproof liner

Cap rail

Plywood with drainage holes

Decking

Privacy screens or fences present large surface areas and should be tastefully designed. Top: Lattice set between posts makes a simple, low-cost screen. Middle: This pleasing arrangement features a mix of 1×6 and 1×1 boards. Bottom: Three layers of 1×2s and 1×1s form a complex and interesting pattern.

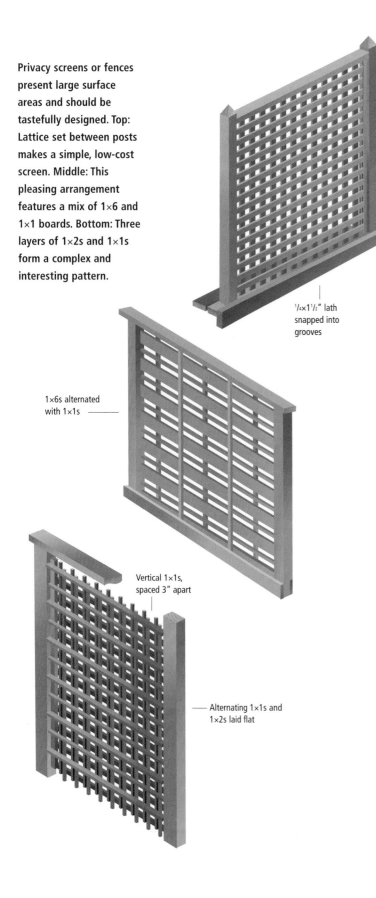

$\frac{1}{4}$×1$\frac{1}{2}$" lath snapped into grooves

1×6s alternated with 1×1s

Vertical 1×1s, spaced 3" apart

Alternating 1×1s and 1×2s laid flat

and in contact with each other, a chemical reaction can occur that produces stains. Be sure to include drainage holes in your liners. For an illustration of a simple planter box, see page 67.

■ *Cooking centers* are increasingly popular. They're short runs of lower cabinets that can withstand outdoor climates. They can hold sinks, gas or electric cooking appliances, and storage compartments for cooking utensils and cleaning supplies.

Because more people enjoy outdoor cooking and entertaining than ever before, the demand for appliances and kitchen utensils has increased. Many manufacturers have responded with cooktops, refrigerators, rotisseries, and other small appliances that are rated for safe use outdoors. These appliances feature stainless steel, anodized aluminum, or enameled bodies that can withstand the rigors of being outdoors.

A cooking center is 34 to 36 inches high and at least 24 inches wide—the same width as a typical lower kitchen cabinet. Cabinets wider than 36 inches are difficult to reach across. Make sure there is at least 18 inches of countertop workspace on either side of a cooktop or sink. Cabinet bodies and countertops should be able to withstand the weather—solid redwood or cedar match the materials usually used for deck construction and are a good choice. Otherwise, cabinets should be made of exterior- or marine-grade plywood.

Use only weatherproof materials for countertops. Solid-surface countertops are durable but might expand and contract with changes in temperature. A professional fabricator should have experience installing solid surface materials in exterior locations. Tile or stone is a good material if it is rated for exterior use. It should be set on a moisture-resistant base such as cement tile backer installed over ¾-inch exterior- or marine-grade plywood. Plastic laminate countertops should not be used.

Left: This small but effective privacy screen was integral to the original design of the deck and railing system. It is supported by extra-long railing posts. This circle-top screen is equally pleasant to look at from the nearby neighbor's point of view.

Sinks require care to ensure that pipes do not freeze. Pipes should be insulated and valves and faucets rated for outdoor use. The best protection against freezing is common sense. When the summer outdoor season is over, drain plumbing lines. If you entertain on a warm fall or spring day, use your indoor kitchen to supply water.

Sensible deck design suggests that cooking centers should be made of materials identical or similar to the materials used to construct the deck, or painted to match the overall scheme.

■ *Privacy screens* block views and establish a sense of enclosure. Privacy screens usually aren't solid—latticework or boards spaced several inches apart are enough to create privacy while permitting air circulation.

Privacy screens can be freestanding fences or extensions of a railing system. When added to a deck, they should be made of the same material as other deck components so that they blend harmoniously with the design. A privacy screen doesn't have to be an enormous wall, either. Sometimes, a well-placed piece of lattice is all that's needed.

If a screen will be between yourself and a close neighbor, remember how the screen will look from the other side. A well-planned screen takes into account appearances from both sides. A good way to add privacy is to build a trellis that supports a climbing plant such as a clematis or trumpet vine. By midsummer, both sides of the trellis should fill in with leafy vines brimming with greenery and blossoms.

Right: Overheads provide unique opportunities to add flair. Cut rafter ends in decorative shapes and add color—such as this blue stain—to add to your deck's personality. Use overheads to grow climbing plants for added shade. Opposite: Arched rafters, simple but stylish posts, and decorative brackets turn this simple arbor into an exotic and inviting outdoor room.

Overheads

Turn your deck into a Greek temple or a romantic cabana with an overhead structure. Overheads provide shade, establish a sense of enclosure, and help define the character and personality of your outdoor room. An overhead usually consists of support posts, rafters, and an open "roof" made of lattice or narrow boards. They are simple structures that don't require a lot of materials and are not expensive to construct.

Pergolas and arbors are common types of overheads. A pergola is attached to a host structure, such as a house. An arbor is free-standing. Both are excellent for supporting climbing greenery such as clematis and

trumpet vines that wrap around posts and work their way across lattice to provide leafy shade during the summer. The intricacy of the lattice pattern also determines how much shade the roof offers. To cut the sun's rays effectively, lattice must be closely spaced—no more than about 2 inches apart.

An overhead must be securely fastened to the deck and well-braced between the posts and joists so that the structure remains rigid in the stiffest winds. This kind of bracing is called knee-bracing or brackets, and is made of short pieces of lumber fastened at an angle.

Building an overhead is a good way to add flair to your deck and to define individual "rooms." Cut the ends of joists in decorative shapes and add curved brackets for stylish touches. Combine your overhead with a trellis or screen to create an outdoor room complete with walls and ceiling.

Above: An imaginative support wall for a soaring overhead structure required expert design skill. Building curved structural members usually requires several thicknesses of wood laminated with exterior glue and painted to hide seams. Right: A pergola doesn't have to be elaborate to be effective. This simple overhead supports a porch swing.

Above: This pergola structure isn't for shade, but it does give a sense of enclosure to the deck. Its sleek design matches the contemporary architecture of the house. Left: Designed to support climbing vines, a rustic overhead is inexpensive to build. The lattice is placed on the south side of the deck, leaving the other half open to sun and sky.

73

Building a Deck

Building a deck could take as little as a week or as much as several months, depending on the size and complexity of the design and on unpredictable events such as weather delays. Despite these variables, most deck construction follows a basic sequence: preparing the site; installing the foundation; building the structural system; adding decking, railings, and stairs; and finishing the job with protective sealers, stains, or paints. While the methods used for each step can vary somewhat from builder to builder, the essential process is straight forward. Being familiar with these steps helps the homeowner make necessary decisions and anticipate problems so that the job proceeds smoothly and efficiently.

Obtaining permits

Any structure attached to a main house—and often any freestanding structure as well—requires a building permit before construction can begin. Permits are issued after a member of the local building or planning department has had a chance to review your plans and evaluate them for safety and structural integrity. If your plans were not produced by an architect, you can have them reviewed by a registered structural engineer before submitting them to a building department. This is an especially helpful step if your deck is complex. Plan to spend $300 to $600 for a structural engineer to review your plans and make suggestions that will address challenges.

Your plans must also meet local "setback" requirements. Setbacks determine the distance that new construction may be from property lines. In certain circumstances, you may be able to apply for a variance that allows you to build within a setback zone. Your application for variance must put forth compelling reasons for the variance, such as the construction of a wheelchair ramp.

Below: Suppress the growth of unwanted vegetation by installing landscaping fabric over the building site. Landscaping fabric prevents weeds and other plants from taking root but allows water to enter the soil. Install the fabric over a sand bed 1 to 2 inches thick, then cover the fabric with gravel to conceal it.

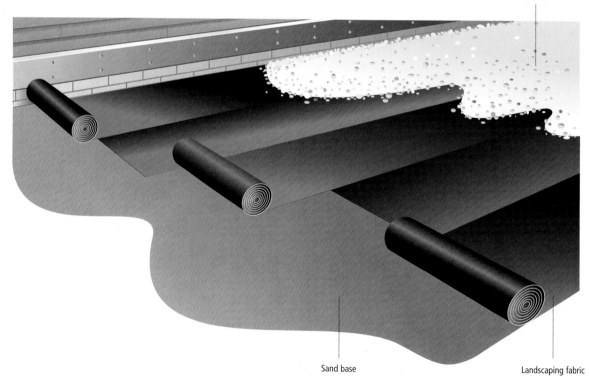

Gravel

Sand base

Landscaping fabric

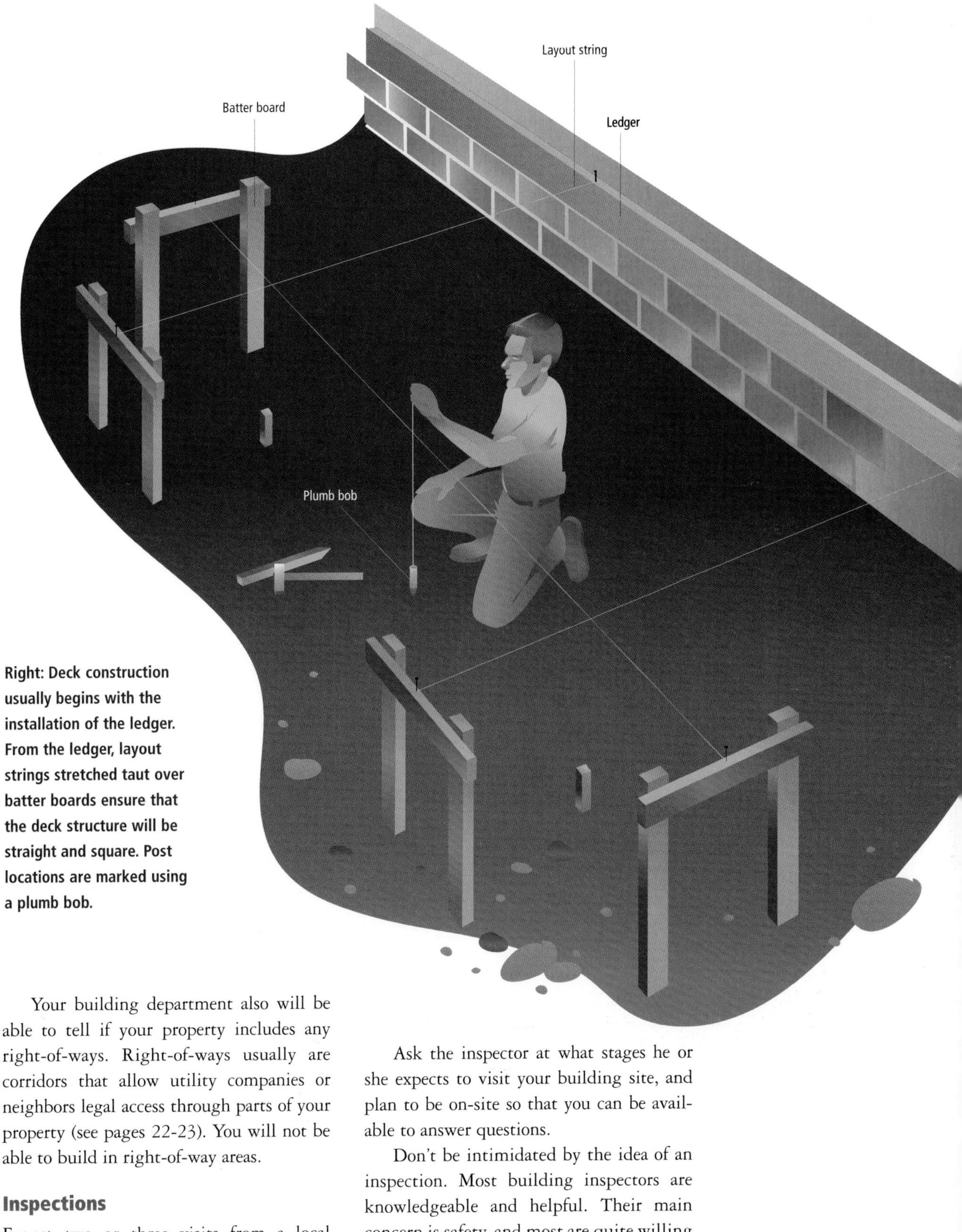

Layout string

Batter board

Ledger

Plumb bob

Right: Deck construction usually begins with the installation of the ledger. From the ledger, layout strings stretched taut over batter boards ensure that the deck structure will be straight and square. Post locations are marked using a plumb bob.

Your building department also will be able to tell if your property includes any right-of-ways. Right-of-ways usually are corridors that allow utility companies or neighbors legal access through parts of your property (see pages 22-23). You will not be able to build in right-of-way areas.

Inspections

Expect two or three visits from a local building inspector during the course of construction. The inspector will examine the structure to ensure it is being built safely and is in compliance with local codes.

Ask the inspector at what stages he or she expects to visit your building site, and plan to be on-site so that you can be available to answer questions.

Don't be intimidated by the idea of an inspection. Most building inspectors are knowledgeable and helpful. Their main concern is safety, and most are quite willing to talk about your specific plans and methods of construction to ensure that your deck project is built soundly and is completed on schedule.

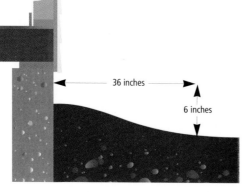

36 inches

6 inches

Right: It's important that the soil next to the foundation is graded so that water drains away from foundation walls. The soil should slope at least 6 vertical inches over a distance of 3 horizontal feet.

Utilities

Notify all utility, cable television, and phone companies about your plans for building a deck. Ask them to mark the underground locations of wires, cables, pipes, and sewer lines. Most companies provide this service for free or a small fee.

Site preparation

Once the plans are finalized and approved by the local building department, work can begin. Any obstructions, such as shrubs, outbuildings, or small trees that are not included in the design, must be removed from the construction site. Soil near the foundation should be graded so that it slopes away from the house at a rate of about 6 vertical inches for every 3 horizontal feet. To suppress the growth of unwanted vegetation underneath the deck, the area should be covered with landscaping fabric (see page 74). First, add a layer of coarse sand for drainage. Then cover the sand with landscaping fabric. Bury the fabric under several inches of gravel. It's more efficient to do this after all footings have been poured.

Foundation work

If the deck is attached to the house, the location of the ledger is marked on the side of the house. Using the ledger location as a reference, the deck is "outlined" with a system of strings pulled taut over staked "batter boards" (see page 75). These string lines establish the edges of the deck and create reference corners. Once the deck is outlined with lines, the strings are used to locate and mark the placement of foundation footings.

After all footing locations are marked, the holes must be dug. For small decks, the holes can be dug with a hand-operated clamshell digger. For larger decks with more than six or seven footing holes, consider renting a power auger. It is an awkward and heavy tool that is not easy to master, but it makes short work of digging holes. A power auger can create a 10-inch-wide hole 42-inches deep in two or three minutes, depending on how hard the soil is.

Main construction

After the preliminary work is completed and the foundation is poured and allowed to cure, the construction of a deck should proceed in a systematic manner. Posts, girders, and joists are installed and braced if necessary. The substructure usually is fastened together with galvanized metal connectors that hold the members securely and provide strength at the joints. Decking is laid over the joists and fastened with galvanized nails or screws. Stairs, railings, and ancillary structures such as overheads are added, and protective sealers, stains, or paints complete the work.

Pools & Spas

Decks are great border areas for swimming pools and spas. Decks make comfortable surfaces for bare feet, and the weather-resistant nature of decking materials make them good surfaces for surrounding a pool or spa. Some synthetic materials (see pages 50–52) include textured surfaces that are ideal for areas that might get wet. You'll need to plan for electrical and plumbing systems and for equipment such as water heaters and filters. If located beneath the deck, equipment should be accessible through a removable or hinged panel.

Decks for pools

Besides being ideal pool surrounds, decks are easily configured to provide areas for sunning and sitting, or to allow access to an above-ground swimming pool. Add privacy screens, overhead shade structures, and cabanas for storing pool toys. Place mechanical equipment, such as pumps and filters, behind a screen to hide them from view.

Cedar and redwood tend to be more splinter-free than pressure-treated wood, although they are more expensive. Because they are constantly exposed to moisture, even weather-resistant poolside decking materials require special care. Coat both sides of decking with a water sealant prior to installation, and plan to reseal the boards annually for top performance.

Remember that most building codes require that pools be surrounded by child-proof fences and gates. Be sure to check with your local building department so that any protective measures are incorporated in your final landscaping and deck-building plans.

Below: Tucked into a corner of the surrounding deck, a poolside sitting area is perfect for sunning and relaxing. It has an unrestricted view of the entire pool—a good idea for keeping an eye on small children.

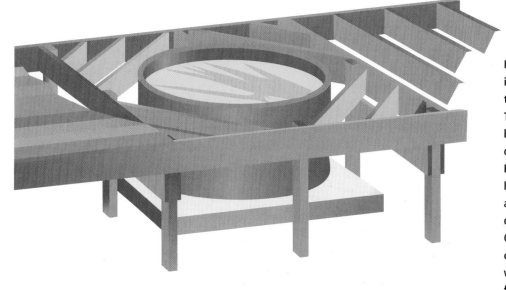

Adding a spa or hot tub

When planning, determine the best location for your spa based on privacy and access to your house, and if you want your tub in a shady or sunny location. If your property offers views, you might want to orient your tub to take advantage of them.

A typical round hot tub is 6 feet in diameter and occupies 30 square feet. A rectangular tub takes up about 48 square feet. You'll want to plan additional space for sitting and unobstructed space at least 36 inches wide that allows you to walk around the tub easily—a total of 100 to 150 square feet of deck space.

When full of water, a hot tub may weigh 2 tons. A typical deck won't support that much weight, so plan for an independent foundation that is engineered by a qualified professional. If you plan to set a tub on an existing deck, restructure the supporting lumber and add a foundation underneath the tub. Some building codes require that tubs be protected by a fence with a childproof gate that restricts access to the tub area. If a fence and gate is not possible, substitute an approved tub cover with childproof latches.

Finishing

Any wood—even pressure-treated wood—will eventually dry out, crack, and turn gray if left exposed to the elements. To protect your investment and to keep your deck looking its best, finish your deck with a clear water-repellant sealer, a stain, or paint. To ensure long life, all surfaces of decking boards should be treated before installation.

Pressure-treated wood used for structural components is resistant to the effects of weathering. If it turns gray and displays some minor cracks, it usually is hidden from view and won't detract from the beauty of your deck. Even so, it's a good idea to finish the ends of structural lumber with a water sealer. The chemicals used to produce pressure-treated lumber sometimes don't soak all the way to the center of the boards.

Treating the ends protects against moisture penetration and ensures the longest possible life for your deck.

Clear finishes

Clear finishes seal wood against moisture and help prolong its beauty. Clear finishes with ultraviolet (UV) blockers help prevent wood from turning gray, but after many years, some graying is inevitable. The best way to keep wood decking looking fresh is to scrub it thoroughly at least once a year with a commercial deck-cleaning agent designed to restore the natural color to the wood. Then seal the decking. Clear finishes with mildewcide are called water-repellent preservatives and help prevent the growth of surface mildew.

Stains

Alter the appearance of a deck with stains or paints especially formulated for use on

decking. Oil-based and water-based stains color the wood and protect it from the effects of moisture and sun. Semitransparent stains let the pattern of the grain show through. Solid stains hide the grain pattern and mask flaws. Test the stain on a scrap piece to make sure you like the final appearance. You can use stain on pressure-treated wood, but because this type of material already is impregnated with a color—either green or brown—it's especially important to test scrap pieces before committing to the final look. Stain can be reapplied every two or three years to freshen the appearance of the deck. Clean the deck thoroughly before reapplying stain.

Paints

Deck paints are specially formulated to withstand weather. As with any paint, exposure to the elements eventually will result in cracking and peeling. Maintaining the appearance of painted surfaces requires periodic scraping, sanding, and recoating.

If specified by the manufacturer, deck paints are resistant to foot traffic and can be used on decking boards. However, this is a harsh test for even the most durable paint. To add color, consider painting railings, fascia, overheads, and built-ins, and finishing decking boards with clear sealers or stains.

Finishing techniques

Decking materials should be dry before painting—but not too dry. Left in the sun without protection, the moisture content of lumber will evaporate quickly, often resulting in split, warped wood. On the other hand, decking materials are often freshly milled and full of moisture, making it difficult for sealers or stains to penetrate into the grain. The key is timing. Wood is ready for finishing if it quickly absorbs a few drops of water sprinkled on its surface.

Before finishing, cover nearby plants, structures, and landscaping features with plastic sheets or drop cloths. Sealers, stains, and paints can be applied with a brush, a

roller, or a sprayer. A roller attached to an extension pole allows you to stand while working, shortening application time. A sprayer coats quickly but sometimes not evenly. Watch for dry spots and recoat them if necessary. Spread puddles with a brush or roller to evenly distribute the finish.

FINISHING BALUSTERS

There's no two ways about it—finishing the individual balusters of a railing system is a tedious, time-consuming job. You can speed up the job with a painter's mitt—a soft, absorbent glove used to apply finish on oddly shaped surfaces. Although a painter's mitt will accelerate the process, controlling the amount of paint is more difficult than with a brush or roller. Be sure to have rags on hand for cleaning up drips, and a brush to smooth out runs.

Avoid painting if the weather is very hot or humid. Either of these conditions can cause the paint to fail to adhere properly. Always use a top-quality primer as the initial coat. Latex primers work well and clean up easily, but oil primers tend to penetrate into the wood more completely, creating a tighter, longer-lasting bond.

Patio Possibilities

Before you effectively plan your patio, you need to know about all of the possibilities to achieve the outdoor living space of your dreams.

At their simplest, patios are areas of your yard that you pave and make into durable, weatherproof spaces for walking or using furniture. With a little imagination and careful planning, however, the simple backyard patio can become a cloistered retreat resplendent with lush plantings and quiet nooks, an extravagant entertainment center with dining areas and extensive seating for guests, or a luxurious spa complete with a hot tub, swimming pool, and shady cabana.

Today's patios are much more than just backyard stations for grilling hot dogs. They are a part of our lifestyle—extending our family rooms into the outdoors to take advantage of nature, sun, and fresh air. They are transitional spaces that blend the best of indoor and outdoor life. More than ever, patios are where we entertain guests, spend time with families, or just get away from it all.

Make the most of your project—and your budget—with careful planning. Good planning includes becoming familiar with the various materials and knowing how patios are built so you can communicate effectively with designers, builders, and other professionals. The result will be a patio that increases the value of your property and is a pleasure for years to come.

Miniature classical temples perched above a garden pond set a tone of elegance for this inviting terrace dining area. The flagstone patio surface contrasts with the stacked stone walls used to surround the pond.

Styles

The size and style of your patio depends on how you plan to use it. It should be a comfortable, well-planned solution to your family's needs. If you entertain often, you'll want an area large enough for guests to comfortably converse, mingle, and dine. If the patio is used only for occasional family barbecues or for relaxing and reading, it can be fairly small. A well-designed patio features different areas that fulfill a variety of expectations. There can be cooking centers, meditative retreats, and outdoor musical stages, often all at once. Listing your primary goals is the first step toward effective planning.

A patio is placed directly on the ground, and the final design often depends on the shape of the terrain. To some extent, land can be altered by machines into a new topography. Of course, extensive site work will affect the cost of your project—expect to pay several thousand dollars for site work that includes grading your land and adding retaining walls. Imaginative design often can solve problems, including uneven land or steep grades.

Before you call in the bulldozers to carve flat areas into your backyard, be sure to consider other options that could be more cost-effective, such as creating a series of smaller, stepped patios or adding a deck that vaults over the landscape. For more information, see Chapter 2, "Evaluating Your Property," beginning on page 20.

Patios don't readily fall into distinct categories, but some styles share basic characteristics. Some common forms:

**Below: Sheltered by an extension of the roof, this covered brick patio offers both sun and shade and can be used if the weather is rainy.
Opposite: A welcoming entry patio leads visitors to the front door.**

Below: An open patio is not sheltered by trees or overhead structures. This one features a washed aggregate surface with insets of troweled concrete. Opposite: Set apart from the house, a getaway patio offers peace and quiet amid a bounty of blossoms. A privacy fence screens views of passersby.

■ *Open patios* are designed to take maximum advantage of sunlight and fresh air. There are few obstructions, and the patio area is usually set apart from large trees and overhangs. They are often found in northern climates, where warming sunlight is valuable. An open patio helps extend enjoyment of the outdoors into spring and fall.

■ *Covered patios* usually are constructed next to a house, where extended eaves or an overhead structure shelters the patio from sun and rain. Often, a portion of the patio floor extends beyond the sheltering roof so that a portion of it is in full sun. A covered patio is much like a porch, except that the flooring is usually masonry installed directly on grade.

■ *Getaway patios* are located away from the house. They are usually small, intimate areas surrounded by plants and landscaping features that provide a sense of privacy. Getaway patios can be open or covered by a simple arbor or gazebo-like structure. They are connected to the main house with a path, and are often built in yards large enough to create separate garden rooms. They include simple furnishings, such as outdoor benches, tables, and chairs.

■ *Poolside patios* provide durable, waterproof surfaces and open areas for sitting or sunning. Slip-resistant surfaces, such as textured

concrete or split-face flagstone, are commonly used for poolside patios.

■ *Entry patios* are built at the front of the house. These public spaces are relaxing and inviting. They are characterized by wide, paved areas and often include landscaping features such as built-in planters, casual seating, and pathways leading to side yards and garages.

REGIONAL STYLES

Patio designs often take their cues from regional influences. Climate, culture, and indigenous plants all play an important role in the design of outdoor living spaces. Regional styles fit well with their surroundings, taking advantage of established methods of construction and materials that originate in the region. This usually means the landscaping components are readily available and cost-effective. An English garden and formal brick patio placed in arid Arizona not only would look out of place, it might be difficult—and expensive—to maintain. For advice about regional materials and plants, consult an experienced professional landscape designer or contractor in your area.

Opposite: Pools and patios naturally go together. To keep the large area of red brick from appearing too monotonous, white bricks have been scattered at random throughout the field. Above: A brick patio surrounded by crunchy gravel echoes the native surroundings of this Arizona home.

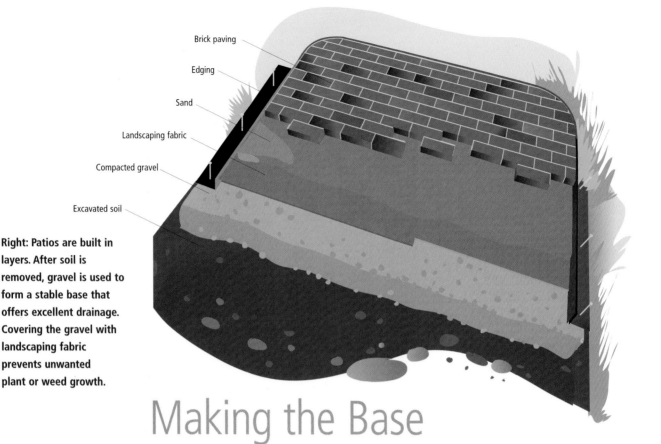

Brick paving

Edging

Sand

Landscaping fabric

Compacted gravel

Excavated soil

Right: Patios are built in layers. After soil is removed, gravel is used to form a stable base that offers excellent drainage. Covering the gravel with landscaping fabric prevents unwanted plant or weed growth.

Making the Base

A patio is made in layers. The bottom layers form a stable base for the top layer of paving material. Careful preparation of the substrate is essential to the long life of the patio. If settling occurs, low spots can develop; large paving materials, such as flagstones or concrete, might crack.

The first step is to a establish satisfactory slope and grade to the project area (see Chapter 2, "Evaluating Your Property," beginning on page 20). To encourage proper drainage, patios should slope away from residences and other buildings at a rate of about

2 vertical inches for every 8 horizontal feet of patio surface.

Once the shape of the patio is laid out, the top layer of sod and dirt is stripped away to a depth of several inches. Protruding roots and stones are removed, and any holes are filled with dirt and tamped smooth. The first layer is about 4 inches of gravel. The gravel is raked flat, then a heavy vibrating tool called a plate compactor or tamp is used to vibrate and pound the gravel into a smooth, firm base. The compacted gravel base forms the foundation for any subsequent patio surfaces. Typical installations include:

■ *Concrete patios* are poured directly on top of the compacted gravel. A 4-inch-thick slab is standard. Large slabs include steel rods, called reinforcement bars, and expansion joints to control cracking.

■ *Brick, stone, or concrete pavers set over concrete* make the most stable, durable, and expensive finished patios. A 4-inch-thick concrete

---

BASE GRAVEL

Gravel used as the base for patio construction typically is called class-5 gravel or 3/4-inch highway gravel. It is a mixture of small irregularly shaped pieces that fit together tightly when tamped. Don't order pea gravel—it won't settle into a firm base. Enough gravel to make a base 4 inches deep for a small, 10x10-foot patio would weigh approximately 5,000 pounds—about 2 1/2 tons.

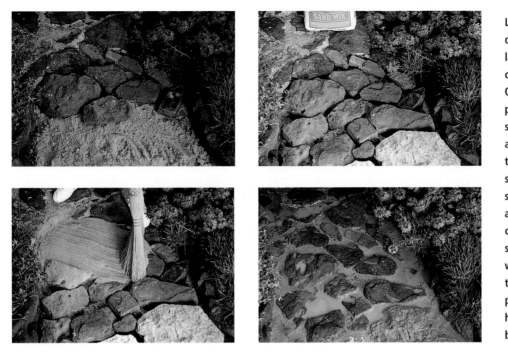

Left: This version of the dry-set method calls for laying stones on a compacted sand base. Once the stones are set in place, pour dry concrete sand mix over the stones and use a broom to sweep the mixture into the spaces between the stones. When the spaces are full and the stones are clean, use a hose to sprinkle—not splash—water over the mix. Once the concrete hardens, the patio stones appear to have been laboriously set by hand in wet concrete.

base is poured over the compacted gravel and allowed to set, then the finish material is applied. Concrete grout holds the paving material in place. See pages 92–105 for more information.

■ *Brick, stone, and concrete pavers set over sand* are called dry-fit. Dry-fit construction requires a layer of landscaping fabric over the compacted gravel to inhibit unwanted growth and a bed of sand over the fabric. Paving material is set on top of the smoothed sand, and sand or dry mortar mix

is spread between the pavers to hold them in place. After being soaked with water from a hose, the mortar mix hardens to lock the paving material into place. Another option is to fill the spaces between the paving material with soil and plant decorative, low-lying groundcover or grass. Dry-set patios are the easiest to construct.

■ *Tiles* are always set on a base of concrete, and mortar grout holds the paving material in place. See pages 106–107 for more information.

Below: Classic patio construction uses bricks set over sand, concrete set over sand, or bricks set over a concrete base—the best and most durable way to build a brick patio.

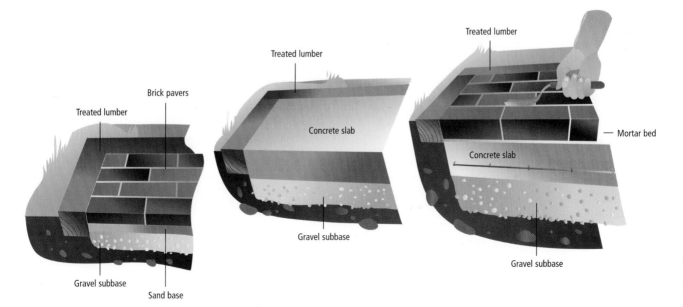

Brick

Warm, earthy brick is a classic material that blends readily with many styles of houses. Its durability makes it a favorite material for outdoor use, and its modular shape is ideal for building many structures, such as patio floors, planters, and garden walls. It comes in many colors and sizes, is moderately priced, and is readily available from home improvement centers, landscaping retailers, and masonry suppliers.

Types of brick

Brick for exterior use comes in many grades and styles. The terms used to describe grades may differ from region to region; however,

two of the most common grades are moderate weather (MW) and severe weather (SW). MW bricks are the less expensive option, although they are more porous and less uniform in size. A porous brick absorbs water. If exposed to low temperatures, the absorbed water can expand as it freezes, causing the brick to chip or break. Although the material is still durable, the freeze/thaw cycle can take its toll over time. In damp conditions, such as perpetually shaded areas, MW brick encourages the growth of moss, a feature some people find charming.

As the name implies, SW bricks are made to withstand temperature extremes and high moisture conditions. They are also

Below: A pergola covered with a trumpet vine creates a shady transition between the interior living spaces of this California home and an expansive brick patio.

more resistant to stains caused by accidental spills of beverages or oily liquids. Here are other kinds of brick:

■ *Common brick* is a general-purpose material that has many uses. Although it is used primarily for walls, it can be used for patios that don't get a lot of foot traffic, and for patios in mild climates that do not have temperature extremes. Common brick can be "wire-cut," meaning it is uniformly square and has a rough texture on its face and smooth edges. "Sandmold" brick often is uneven in shape but has a smooth face that is easy to clean.

■ *Paving brick* is made with a dense clay and is fired at extremely high temperatures to produce a product that is especially hard and resistant to moisture. Paving brick is the most durable brick and is a good choice for patio surfaces.

Above: Dark red brick is the perfect paving material for a Mediterranean-style courtyard added to this San Diego home. The heavy chairs and tables reflect Spanish design influence.

Right: Salvaged brick is the perfect complement to a renovated 1870s brick house. Nestled under the shade of big trees, this cozy patio recalls gracious living of a century ago. Below: Using bricks of different colors, the owners of this modest suburban house created an arresting pattern for their backyard brick patio. Planning interesting brick patterns is not difficult, but it's best to work out possibilities on paper beforehand.

■ *Used brick* is salvaged from demolished buildings. It has a worn, rustic character that many people find attractive. Because of the added labor of salvage work, it usually costs more than other types of brick. Because old brick usually has had many years of exposure to the elements, it might not be as hard and durable as newer ones. One strategy for using older brick is to buy enough to have replacements if individual bricks crumble or break. Another idea is to make ancillary structures, such as walls and planters, from used brick and buy a paver of matching color for use throughout the patio field. Used brick might not be uniform in size, and it will vary in thickness from 2½ inches to 3 inches.

■ *Clinker bricks* have imperfections caused by improper firing methods. Defects include irregular shapes, scorch marks, and pitting. Some suppliers offer inexpensive clinker bricks for use as decorative borders or as accents distributed randomly through a field of normal bricks.

Brick patterns

The modular shape of brick is ideal for forming patterns. Over the years, many classic patterns have been developed that are familiar to installers. Some patterns, such as the pinwheel pattern shown at center right, require the time-consuming cutting of individual bricks. For the most part, the layout and installation of various patterns is straightforward. Patterns also can be mixed to create custom decorative layouts.

Irregular shapes and curves usually add to the cost of any patio project. Curves mean cutting bricks, which adds to the time required for construction. Bricks and other types of masonry can be precisely cut with a water or tub saw—a large, circular blade made especially for slicing masonry. A flow of water onto the blade helps reduce friction and dust during cutting. Do-it-yourselfers can rent a water saw at a rental shop.

Running Bond

Herringbone

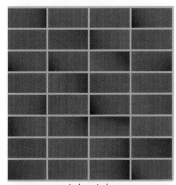

Jack on Jack

Pinwheel

Basket Weave

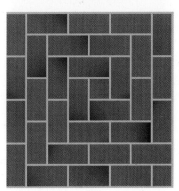

Spiral

Right: Native flagstone set in concrete creates a handsome, rustic patio that wends through this Texas garden area. This patio was built using the dry-set techniques described on page 91.

Stone

For unmatched natural beauty, few patio materials are as compelling as stone. It comes in many textures and colors and works remarkably well with a variety of architectural styles. It is available in all areas of the country as rough pieces of flagstone and as cut tiles manufactured in uniform dimensions and thicknesses.

Stones vary in hardness, depending on where they were quarried and the geological forces that made them. Some types of sandstone, for example, are nearly as hard and scratch-resistant as marble. Others can be dented with a fingernail.

Stones also vary in porosity—their ability to absorb water. A porous stone absorbs water. During cold weather, this water can freeze and expand, damaging the stone. Stones with a low rate of absorption are more durable and long-lasting in outdoor environments than more porous stones. Always ask your dealer about the hardness, durability, and porosity of different kinds of stone.

Flagstone

The term flagstone refers to the many types and regional varieties of flat, natural stones taken from quarries and cut or broken into individual pieces of various sizes, shapes, and thicknesses. Some of the most common are granite, sandstone, limestone, slate, bluestone, and quartzite.

Split-face flagstone, sometimes called cleft-face, presents a rough, uneven surface and has a rustic appearance. Honed-face flagstone has been smoothed by machine and has a more refined look, although the texture is still rougher than concrete or tile. Flagstone comes in many colors, and the same type of stone taken from different quarries can exhibit dramatically different hues and tones.

When choosing flagstone, be sure to examine types thoroughly for the color that complements your design. Be prepared to pay a premium price for natural flagstone— it can be considerably more expensive than common brick or concrete.

Patio flagstone ranges in size from about 6 inches to 2 feet across, and ½ inch to 2 inches thick. Larger pieces are usually available but can be too heavy for workers to handle without mechanical equipment, such as a backhoe or front-end loader.

Because of their irregular shapes, setting flagstone is a specialized installation. If you will be hiring out the installation, try to find experienced installers.

Stone tiles

Almost any type of stone can be cut and shaped by machine into uniform sizes and thicknesses to form stone tiles. Tumbled marble and slate tiles are two of the most popular. Sandstone, limestone, and granite are also readily available as tiles of uniform dimension and thickness. Because of the

Left: Cutting stones directly into sod lets grasses or groundcovers grow between the stones. Leave a gap of several inches between stones so that plant roots are not restricted and water can penetrate the soil.

Above: Big pieces of red Colorado sandstone form this shady sitting patio in a remote corner of a backyard. Fitting large pieces of stone takes a lot of patience and muscle. Right: This patio of cut and honed bluestone is called "The Dance Floor" by its owners because of its smooth, even surface.

labor required to cut stone, expect to pay premium prices for stone tiles.

Like all tiles, stone tile cannot be set directly on a dry-fit sand bed. The sand is too flexible, and eventually the tiles will crack and break. Stone tiles must be set on a base of poured concrete and grout used to fill the spaces between tiles.

Rocks and pebbles

Other types of naturally occurring stones include rounded river rocks and pebbles. These types of stones have been worn smooth by water or by glacial movement, and they are found throughout North America. Their diameters usually range from 1 inch to 8 inches. These types of rocks are extremely durable, moisture-resistant, and inexpensive. Because of their rounded shape, however, they can cause problems when used as patio surfaces. Smaller varieties can be set in concrete slabs to create a highly textured surface or as loose fill around larger pieces of flagstone. Larger pieces can be used as decorative accents along the edges of patios and walkways.

Concrete

Concrete is an inexpensive, versatile material that makes durable, smooth-surfaced patios. It can be formed into a variety of sizes and shapes, including curves, and it works well combined with other surfacing materials, such as decorative edges made of rock or tile. It can be finished in many colors and textures, or stamped while still wet to resemble other materials, such as brick or stone. Properly prepared concrete patios will last a lifetime with little maintenance.

A drawback of concrete is its tendency to crack. Over time, temperature extremes and freeze/thaw cycles put stress on a concrete slab. Diligent concrete contractors plan slabs carefully, using reinforcing wire and steel bars inside the slab and control joints throughout the field to prevent cracking. Control joints are seams about ⅜-inch wide that are filled with nonporous felt or pressure-treated wood. Control joints allow the slab to expand and contract without cracking. Control joints are spaced at least 10 feet apart. When planning a concrete patio, be sure to consult with your concrete contractor or designer about the location of control joints so they fit into your design.

Pre-mixed concrete arrives in a truck. The driver will try to park as close as possible to the construction site to simplify delivery of the concrete. However, trucks can be equipped with pumps that allow the concrete to be delivered through long hoses to nearly anywhere on the site.

Surface finishes

Slab surfaces are finished until flat and smooth with tools called floats and trowels. However, perfectly smooth concrete surfaces

Below: Every child knows the delight of poking into wet concrete. Here, some young-at-heart grown-ups have made a decorative border by pressing rounded rocks into concrete while it's still wet.

Left: Tiny pebbles pressed into wet concrete give the illusion of flagstones separated by lines of grout. Below: Classically elegant, this concrete patio features a washed aggregate surface that has been divided into squares by borders of stone set into smoothed concrete.

molds are available at home improvement centers and concrete supply shops. You can use the molds to create custom patterns.

Adding color

Coloring concrete slabs is becoming a more popular way to add design flair to this basic material. There are three methods: *integral colors, dry-shake hardeners,* and *chemical stains.* Integral colors and dry-shake hardeners are used on new concrete. To color an existing slab, use chemical stains.

Coloring concrete is not an exact science. Results vary from slab to slab depending on the composition of the concrete, the temperature when it is poured, and how much time elapses between the finishing of the slab and the application of the coloring technique. Many concrete contractors are not familiar with the techniques. If possible, seek out a contractor who has had experience applying color to concrete, and ask to see samples before committing to a specific technique.

■ *Integral colors* are raw mineral oxide pigments that are added to pre-mixed concrete before it is delivered. The method costs more and the colors are not as vibrant as other techniques. However, the color extends through the entire thickness of the slab, rather than just its surface. Chips and cracks won't expose uncolored concrete, making the technique ideal for patios and exterior walkways. To design color combinations, you must order separate batches of concrete and conduct individual pours.

Some pre-mix suppliers don't offer colored concrete, saying it stains the interiors of the delivery truck mixers and could contaminate the next batch of concrete with unwanted color.

■ *Dry-shake hardeners,* also known as *dust-on colors,* are applied to the wet surface of a freshly poured slab. The colors are a mixture of silica, pigment, and cement that is sprinkled onto the slab and then worked into the concrete with a trowel. The color usually extends to a depth of about $1/8$ inch. Because the coloring agent is concentrated on top of the slab, colors are vibrant. A wide range of hues is available. Dry-shake hardeners tend

Above: The owner of this patio in San Diego decided to jazz it up with concrete stain. Before selecting colors, he worked out the design on paper. When he was satisfied, he bought the appropriate hues and brushed the stain on by hand. A gallon of concrete stain costs about $25 and covers about 200 square feet.

can be slippery when wet and are not the best choices for outdoor living areas. Here are some ways to add texture to the finished surface:

■ *Exposed aggregate surfaces* are some of the most common finish treatments. There are two basic methods. *Seeded* aggregates are created by sprinkling small, colored stones over the top of the concrete when it is still wet. This makes a rustic, pebbly texture that is especially good for wet areas, such as around swimming pools. *Floated* aggregate finishes are created by rubbing the surface of the wet concrete repeatedly with a wooden float. The action of the float brings small stones to the surface. A gentle washing of the top of the slab after floating further exposes the imbedded aggregate. Seeding techniques usually involve round pebbles; the aggregate exposed with a float usually is rougher and sharper-edged, and provides superior traction.

■ *Broom-finished surfaces* are swept with a stiff bristle broom while the concrete is damp. The sweeping creates tiny ridges that greatly increase traction. Use broom finishing to create subtle patterns of texture, such as checkerboards and random swirls.

■ *Stamping* wet concrete with a plastic mold leaves impressions that, when dry, resemble brick, tile, or stone. Inexpensive plastic

Left: A patio of sandstone pavers looks great set against a pool designed with gentle curves that mimic nature's own swimming holes. The poolside walls are made of quarried limestone salvaged from an old house.

to harden the surface of the slab, making it less porous and more impervious to weather.

■ *Chemical staining,* sometimes referred to as *color etching,* uses a blend of muriatic acid and metallic salts that is applied to the surface of a fully cured slab—new concrete should cure for 30 to 45 days before stains are applied. The acid breaks down the surface glaze to a depth of about $\frac{1}{16}$ inch. Either a water-based or solvent-based stain is applied by rolling, sponging, and splattering—each produces a different look.

Buy chemical stains at hardware stores, paint stores, or home improvement centers. You'll find them in a variety of pastels and deeper organic colors such as olives, browns, and golds, but the true final color depends on the age and chemical composition of the existing slab. The technique can be used by do-it-yourselfers, but the slab must be thoroughly cleaned before application. Be careful when handling etching materials, and be sure to wear safety goggles and acid-resistant gloves.

Concrete Pavers

Strong, durable concrete pavers are ideal for patio surfaces. They are made from dense, cast concrete that is pressed into molds at high pressure, resulting in an exceptionally tough paving material that resists breaking, staining, and the effects of weather.

Concrete pavers are about 1½ to 2½ inches thick—thinner than regular bricks—and come in many shapes and textures to match any design scheme. You'll find them as squares, rectangles, circles, diamonds, hexagons, octagons, and crescents. Many of the shapes are designed to be used in combinations to create interesting patterns. Some squares and rectangles have slightly beveled sides made for circular patterns. Others are interlocking; they fit together like pieces of a puzzle, creating an extremely stable surface. Concrete pavers usually cost less than brick or stone.

Paver colors tend to be muted, earthtoned shades of gray, tan, red, and green. Specify one color or vary your patterns even more by specifying several colors of the same style of paver. When shopping, examine the surfaces closely. The pigment layer in some

Below: A mix of square and rectangular concrete pavers in various shades of gray gives this patio the appearance of being made of cut stone. Pavers can be dry-set or set in a mortar base. The pavers in this example cover a concrete slab.

pavers is very thin. When scratched or chipped, the gray concrete beneath shows through; you might decide to reject these pavers. Surface textures vary: Some are smooth; others have rough, aggregate surfaces or are made to look like brick, stone, adobe, or cobblestone.

Many pavers have beveled edges that create patterns of light and shadow. When designing your patio, remember that small pavers can create very busy patterns when used in large areas.

Concrete pavers are made especially to withstand heavy loads. Some pavers are designated as "road weight;" they can endure the weight of vehicles without cracking and can be used for driveways. If you like the pattern and color of a road-weight paver, and are willing to pay the slightly higher prices, they make excellent patio surfaces.

Above: Concrete pavers are cast in many shapes, including wedges of various widths used to create circles and curved, flowing designs. Left: Made to look like brick, these cast-concrete paving squares are faster to install, less expensive, and more durable than traditional brick.

Right: Unglazed quarry tile has a slightly rough, slip-resistant texture that is a good choice for pool surrounds. With their rounded-over, finished edges, bullnosed tiles are perfect for lining the perimeter of the pool.

Tile

Captivating and intriguing, tile has extraordinary beauty and a limitless potential for pattern and color. Tile rated for use outdoors is durable, moisture-resistant, and requires little maintenance, so it's an excellent choice for patios. Ceramic flooring tile is readily available in varieties that complement almost any architectural style and type of design. Tiles must be set on a concrete base. Setting tile involves considerable labor, which adds to the overall cost.

Rating tiles for floors

Floor tiles usually are harder and more durable than tiles made for walls or countertops. Also, floor tiles have different degrees of resistance to abrasion, slippage, staining, and breakage. For patios, a nonporous, slip-resistant tile is usually preferred. When selecting tiles for outdoor floors, always check the manufacturer's recommendations.

The American National Standards Institute (ANSI) has developed ratings that help determine the proper tile for various uses. ANSI has established four categories that rate tiles by their ability to absorb water, their porosity. These categories essentially reflect how a tile is manufactured. Tiles made with lower temperatures and shorter kiln times tend to be softer and more porous, making the tile more susceptible to staining or breakage. Tiles fired at higher temperatures and for longer periods are hard and dense, and more resistant to abrasion and stains. The four categories include:

■ *Impervious*—absorbs less than 0.5 percent of its weight in water. These kinds of tiles can stand heavy traffic and very wet conditions. They withstand freezing and are ideal for all-weather outdoor use. This type is the best choice for patios.

■ *Vitreous*—absorbs more than 0.5 percent but less than 3 percent. A vitreous tile is a good all-around indoor flooring choice and is suitable for bathrooms or kitchens.

■ *Semivitreous*—more than 3 percent but less than 7 percent. Because a semivitreous tile can stain, it might require sealing before it can be used in very wet areas such as kitchens or baths. Be sure to check the manufacturer's recommendations.

■ *Nonvitreous*—more than 7 percent. Usually not recommended for floors.

Types of flooring tiles

Floor tiles usually are either glazed or unglazed. Both types can be used for patio flooring, but glazed tiles tend to be slippery when wet, making them a poor choice as an outdoor tile. However, they can be used as accents and borders. Unglazed tiles take their characteristic earth tones from the color of the fired clay itself. Glazed tiles have a colored ceramic coating that is bonded to the tile in a kiln at high temperatures.

Tiles are identified in a variety of ways. Sometimes, different names are given to the same type of tile, depending on regional or historical influences. Here are the most common names for types of tile:

■ *Quarry tile* is a tough, durable tile ideal for patio flooring. It's made of a mixture of clay and shale that is fired at high temperatures. Quarry tile is usually unglazed and is available in a variety of natural earth tones, such as browns, dark reds, yellows, and grays. Slight variations in the color of each tile give each floor unique characteristics.

Quarry tile has a slightly textured, skid-resistant surface that makes it an appropriate choice for outdoors. It is stain-resistant, but most manufacturers recommend sealing quarry tile to prevent discoloration.

■ *Terra-cotta* often refers to the look of a tile rather than specific properties or process of manufacture. Generally, terra-cotta tiles are thought of as being rustic, handmade tiles imported from Mexico or Europe with uneven edges, pitting, and other surface imperfections that give them distinctive character. Today, however, they can also be purchased with smooth, even surfaces and well-defined edges. Terra-cotta tiles usually are unglazed and have the same natural clay colors—ocher and umber—as quarry tile. Because of the many different techniques used to produce terra-cotta tiles, they vary in price and quality. Most are rated as semivitreous. Always check the manufacturer's recommendations before specifying terra-cotta tiles for a patio.

■ *Porcelain floor tiles* are made at very high temperatures that make them extremely hard and stain resistant. Porcelain tiles with slip-resistant textures are an excellent choice for patio floors. Unglazed porcelain tiles are made with clay and feldspar that is often mixed with mineral oxide pigments to produce beautiful, muted colors.

■ *Glazed ceramic floor tile* has a ceramic coating that's bonded to a clay body during a kiln firing. The glazing can be virtually any color or texture imaginable, and it presents enormous freedom of design. Because the manufacturing process is usually simple, glazed tiles are relatively inexpensive.

Glazing helps tiles resist stains and moisture, but check to see if the manufacturer has provided a hardness rating for the glaze that will help you determine whether it is a good flooring material. A rating of 1 to 4 means the glaze is not hard and the tile should be used on walls only. A rating of 5 or 6 can be used for low-traffic areas. Higher ratings indicate the tile is a good choice for most flooring installations.

Below: Terra-cotta tiles have a rustic texture and an informal appearance. These reddish tiles are a good choice for an informal courtyard at the back of a Spanish colonial-style house in San Diego.

Right: A gravel patio is easy to install, inexpensive, and requires little maintenance. It even sounds great when walked upon. To inhibit the growth of weeds and other unwanted vegetation, install the gravel over a layer of landscaping fabric.

Loose Materials and Combinations

Loose materials—gravel, river rock, and wood chips—provide interesting textures and colors for patio surfaces. They make good filler materials when used with solid surfaces, such as concrete and brick. Loose materials offer good drainage and are an inexpensive way to give your patio a unique look. Some types of loose materials make excellent pathways and transitional surfaces between patios and other areas of your yard, such as gardens. They are usually sold by the bag at home improvement centers, landscape suppliers, and lumberyards. Here are some common types:

■ *Gravel* is obtained from natural deposits. A load of gravel includes pieces that range in size from about 1 inch across to ¼ inch or less in diameter. Gravel usually contains dust that eventually washes out of the upper layers of a gravel bed. It packs well and forms a stable base, but has sharp edges that are not comfortable to bare feet.

■ *Crushed rock* is produced by machine. Rocks are broken into pieces and sorted according to size so that the final product has a uniform appearance and color. It does not pack as well as gravel, but it forms a stable base. Like gravel, crushed rock has sharp edges that are uncomfortable for bare feet.

■ *River rock* has a smooth, rounded appearance. It varies in size from 4 inches in diameter to less than ½ inch. The smaller material should be used for patios. River rock does not pack well and remains loose, but its rounded texture is comfortable to walk on.

■ *Volcanic or lava rock* is lightweight and rough-textured. It usually is dark red or charcoal black and comes in 1- to 2-inch diameters. It forms a very stable fill because its rough edges defy movement, but it is not comfortable for bare feet. Volcanic rock is easy to handle.

■ *Wood chips and bark nuggets* are usually waste products from wood processing mills. They are made from different species of wood and initially appear in a variety of colors, but eventually they all turn gray. Because they are lightweight, they tend to scatter easily in stiff winds. They are also biodegradable, so they will require occasional maintenance to restore loft to decomposed areas. They are inexpensive and easy to obtain.

Because they tend to spread out over time, loose materials should be contained within borders made of brick, stone, or wood. Plastic borders, available at home improvement centers, bend easily to form curves. To control the growth of weeds and other unwanted vegetation, install loose materials over a layer of landscaping fabric.

Above: A patio of honed slate is especially handsome when set off by a border of red brick. Because these materials have different thicknesses, the beds that support them must be carefully measured before installation. Left: This simple, low-cost checkerboard pattern was made by alternating 3-foot concrete squares with squares of reddish granite gravel.

Right: Grouted together to form a design that is both formal and rustic, 1-foot square quarry tiles give way to a random pattern of flagstone pieces.
Below: Various masonry materials are surprisingly compatible, as demonstrated by honed marble tiles paired with common brick.

Combining materials

Combine different patio materials to create interesting, one-of-a-kind textures and designs. The idea works best if materials are similar in thickness and can share the same base. Otherwise, the finished surface will be uneven, with one material protruding awkwardly and dangerously above the other.

One solution is to use materials suitable for installation over a sand bed—brick and stone are good examples. By making the sand bed 1½ to 2 inches thick, you can custom set each piece of material, making sure it is level with others by digging out or adding sand as needed. Unfortunately, this method is time-consuming and labor-intensive. Instead, you can install materials side-by-side on beds of different thicknesses. One of the best substrates for combining

Left: For interesting, one-of-a-kind patios, concrete is the ultimate media mixer. Here, odd-shaped pieces of gray concrete are bedded with pebbles, seashells, and ceramic tiles in a brownish concrete mortar base to form an expressive and whimsical sunburst pattern.

materials is concrete. For best results, prepare a concrete slab patio and imbed materials in the wet concrete, rather than prearranging the materials and grouting between them. However, concrete is not a forgiving material and it dries quickly. You will not have a lot of time to install materials and create intricate designs before the concrete starts to harden. Any mistakes or misalignments could become permanent.

MATERIAL	DURABILITY	COLOR CHOICES	BASE REQUIRED	EASE OF INSTALLATION	COST— MATERIAL ONLY
BRICK	Good	Organic reds, tans, browns, grays	Dry-fit over gravel and sand base, or mortared over concrete	Dry-fit is relatively easy; mortared requires skill	$3–$4 per square foot
FLAGSTONE	Good	Reds, cream, yellows, grays, dark blues, browns, some variations	Dry-fit over gravel and sand base, or mortared over concrete	Dry-fit is relatively easy; mortared requires skill	$3–$4 per square foot
QUARRY TILE	Excellent	Organic reds, tans, browns, grays	Mortar and grout over concrete	Requires skill	$1–$2 per square foot
CONCRETE SLAB	Excellent	Dull gray; can be colored	Gravel and sand base	Simple but labor intensive	About $1 per square foot
CONCRETE PAVER	Excellent	Organic reds, tans, browns, grays	Dry-fit over gravel and sand base, or mortared over concrete	Dry-fit is relatively easy; mortared requires skill	$2–$3 per square foot
UNGLAZED CERAMIC TILE	Excellent	Unlimited	Mortar and grout over concrete	Requires skill	$3–$25 per square foot

Patios can include many beautiful and functional elements. Additional structures such as benches, planters, privacy screens, and cooking centers make your patio more liveable and give your patio flexibility when entertaining. Stairs and paths lead you to other areas of your yard. Hot tubs and spas add enjoyment and luxurious comfort. All these components help you to get the most from your outdoor spaces.

Providing shade

Shade is always a primary concern for outdoor living spaces. Too little shade can make a patio unbearable in the summer sun; too much shade can create cool, damp conditions that can take the fun out of spring or fall. Balancing shade with your needs is an important part of patio planning.

Two basic ways incorporate shade into your design. One is with deciduous trees—the kind that lose their leaves in fall. A deciduous tree leafs out and offers generous amounts of shade in the summer. In the spring when leaves are beginning to grow and in the autumn when leaves fall, more sun can reach patio surfaces.

Taking advantage of deciduous plantings usually requires that the patio be near a fully mature tree. Trees located to the west of the patio will provide the most relief during the late afternoon and early evening—the hottest parts of the day. Because the sun is directly overhead in the summer, trees to the south must be close so the branches overhang the patio surface and offer shade during the middle of the day.

Another way to create shade is to build an overhead—a pergola or an arbor. Both of these structures provide cooling shade with a network of rafters and lattice boards supported by posts. To provide flexibility, build an overhead so that it covers only a portion of your patio space. This way, you can move

Below: A simple pergola made of 2×8 rafters topped with flat 2×4s casts cooling shade on this patio dining area.

Left: Vinyl plastic lattice makes an ideal privacy screen. It's tough, durable, and never needs repainting.

in and out of sunlight to suit your comfort. Pergolas and arbors also are used to define certain portions of your patio, creating small "rooms" with distinct personalities.

The posts of a structure such as a pergola or arbor require connections to the patio surface. Common terms used to describe these connecting points are "integral" and "mechanical."

Integral connections are part of the original design and can include components such as treated wooden posts that extend through the patio surface and are imbedded in concrete, or posts made entirely of masonry. Mechanical connections usually are wooden posts fastened to the patio with galvanized metal brackets. Mechanical connectors allow a pergola or arbor to be built after the original patio surface is completed.

Privacy screens

Privacy screens block views and provide a sense of enclosure. Screens usually aren't solid—an open latticework or boards spaced several inches apart are enough to create privacy while allowing the air to circulate.

Privacy screens can be freestanding fences or attached to the patio by integral or mechanical connections (see "Providing shade" on page 112). They should harmonize with other elements of your design. When constructing privacy fences along the perimeter of your property, be sure to check with your local building department. In some areas, building codes restrict the height of fences. If your screen is between yourself and a close neighbor, consider how the screen will look from the other side.

A well-planned privacy screen takes into account appearances from either side. A stylish way to add privacy is to build a trellis that supports a climbing plant such as a clematis or trumpet vine. The trellis structure affords a measure of privacy during the early part of the outdoor season. By midsummer, it should fill in with leafy vines and colorful blossoms.

Planters

Built-in planters add dimension and texture to the flat plane of a patio. They can define the edges of the patio space and can be used to divide large patios into individual rooms and seating areas. Filled with plants, they add dashes of color and help soften the hard edges of an all-masonry patio.

Integrate the appearance of a planter with your patio by building it from the same materials used for the patio floor. For annual or perennial flowers, make planters 8 to 12 inches deep. Planters for shrubs should be 18 to 24 inches deep. Fill the bottoms of the planters with 2 to 3 inches of pea gravel to ensure good drainage. The bottom of the planters should have drainage that extends to the soil or compacted gravel base. Masonry planters are waterproof, so adding a liner isn't necessary.

Stairs

Building stairs inside a house is tricky enough; building them in the ground from cement or other masonry materials takes careful planning and precise measurements to ensure the finished steps are safe, attractive, and will stand up to the elements.

Patio steps are built one of two ways. For dry-fit steps, the edges of the stairs are formed with a solid, rigid material such as pressure-treated lumber or railroad ties. The insides of the forms are then partially filled with sand. The sand is used as a base for bricks, stones, or concrete pavers.

Longer-lasting steps are made of concrete. After excavating the area where the steps are located, wood forms will be built.

Below: This well-designed patio has features that blend function and aesthetics, using stone planter boxes, concrete pedestals that support posts for an overhead pergola, and a built-in trellis.

Left: The owners of this Indianapolis property built this raised patio themselves, using black concrete pavers for a surface material. The leading edges of these broad steps feature rounded-over bullnose tiles.

Concrete then will be poured into the forms and allowed to cure. If the steps are to be plain concrete, scratch the surfaces with a broom or wash them to expose the aggregate and provide better traction. Otherwise, cover the steps with brick, stone, tile, or concrete pavers. The thickness of the finish material must be taken into account when calculating the proportions of the stairs.

When using a natural material, such as flagstone, sort the pieces carefully so that they have uniform thickness and are free of irregularities, such as depressions or ridges, that might be a tripping hazard.

Spas

Spas are popular amenities for patios. Prefabricated spas are made from acrylic or fiberglass in a variety of shapes and sizes. Concrete spas are custom-formed from spray-on concrete called gunite—a mixture of hydrated cement and aggregates that has adhesive properties. When sprayed on a wall, gunite sticks and sets in place. Many swimming pools are made from gunite.

Spas can be set above or below grade. Above-grade installations are the easiest and least expensive. The spa usually is set in a raised section of concrete block that's veneered to match surrounding patio materials and has steps to access the spa. Controls for the spa are housed in the block surround.

STAIR RISE AND RUN

For safety, stairs should have uniform rise and run: That is, the height and length should be the same from step to step so that there are no surprises to trip over. Also, the rise and run must be in proportion. Building codes specify a typical step to have a rise of about 7 inches, and a run of 12 inches. Shortening the run of the steps to accommodate a steeper grade means increasing the rise. Conversely, long runs require short rises. Building codes do not allow stairs to be too steep. However, they are lenient when it comes to constructing stairs with especially long runs.

Riser   Tread

Spas also require heavy-duty foundations to support their considerable weight when filled with water and people. Below-grade installations allow the top lip of the spa to be flush with, or close to, the patio flooring. The excavation hole must be large enough to contain the spa and any mechanical and plumbing systems. For gunite spas, the excavation hole becomes the rough form for the finished spa.

Finishing & Maintenance

Many kinds of stone and unglazed tiles are porous. Depending on the type of material, their surfaces absorb water. This porosity means they can be stained by spills, dirt, wet leaves, and rusting metal, such as grills or tools. To prevent staining and keep patio surfaces looking fresh, stone and tile surfaces should be finished with the right kind of sealer. Your tile or stone supplier should be able to make specific sealer recommendations for particular types of materials available in your area.

Bricks, concrete, and concrete pavers are impervious to the effects of moisture and temperature fluctuations. Sealers usually are not recommended. The exceptions include eating areas where spills can occur; a sealer can help prevent stains, especially from colored liquids such as fruit juices or wine. Also, a sealer could help deepen the color of the masonry. Because the colors of brick and concrete pavers can fade with time, a sealer can be used to restore and enhance colors.

Sealers are either surface-type or penetrating, and can be water-based or solvent-based. Surface-type sealers resist moisture and stains well. They have a higher degree of sheen than penetrating sealers, but surface-type sealers must be stripped off and replaced every two or three years. Penetrating sealers have a softer sheen,

TREATING EFFLORESCENCE

Efflorescence is a naturally occurring white haze that sometimes appears on the surface of brick, concrete, concrete pavers, and certain kinds of stone. Chemically speaking, it is caused when lime or calcium oxide in the masonry is dissolved by water—rain, dew, or overspray from a sprinkler system—and carried to the surface of the paving material. There, it reacts with carbon dioxide in the air to form a chalky haze of calcium carbonate. When the masonry is wet, the haze seems to disappear. When dry, it reappears.

Efflorescence is not harmful to the masonry, but it can be an unsightly nuisance. Some of it can be removed with a stiff wire brush and soap and water. Be careful, however. A vigorous scrubbing can scratch some kinds of brick. If scrubbing doesn't work, use a weak solution of 1 part muratic acid (available at hardware stores) to 20 parts water, scrubbing the area with a brush and rinsing well with water. Commercially prepared solutions for removing efflorescence can be purchased at masonry supply stores.

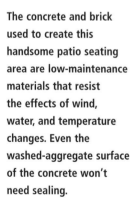

The concrete and brick used to create this handsome patio seating area are low-maintenance materials that resist the effects of wind, water, and temperature changes. Even the washed-aggregate surface of the concrete won't need sealing.

might darken the color of the material slightly, and, over time, they allow it to develop a patina. Penetrating sealers can be maintained by simply applying a fresh coat. Mortar-set materials usually are set and grouted before sealing. To prevent grout from staining the surface of the masonry, the paving materials are set in place and then coated with a water-soluble grout sealer. After the grout is applied and has cured, the grout sealer is washed off. Then the entire floor surface is sealed, including the grout.

Cleaning and stain removal

One of the best features of patio floors is their low maintenance. Sweep floors frequently to remove grit that may scratch the surface. Damp mop ceramic tile once or twice a month, changing water often. Wipe up any spills immediately. Stubborn stains should be scrubbed with a nylon pad or soft bristle brush using a neutral pH detergent cleaner. Do not use steel wool to clean tiles. For persistent stains, try using a nonflammable, nonacidic solvent cleaner, such as a window-cleaning product. If that doesn't work, use a solution of 20 percent phosphoric acid (available at hardware stores) and water. Always use rubber gloves and protect your eyes from accidental splashes when using any acidic cleaning solutions. For more information, check the telephone book Yellow Pages listings under "Tile—Ceramic—Contractors & Dealers" for advice on tile cleaning and cleaning products.

Because grout is porous, it usually needs to be cleaned more often than the surrounding tiles. Grout can be cleaned using a soft-bristle toothbrush and the same techniques described above. For exceptionally stubborn stains or unsightly grout, you might have to remove the grout and replace it.

Spills on brick, concrete, and concrete pavers should be cleaned as soon as possible to prevent staining. Blot the spill with paper towels or a dry cotton cloth. Soak the soiled area for several minutes with a neutral pH detergent cleaner, then scrub the stain with a nylon pad or soft bristle brush and hot water. Several treatments might be necessary to completely remove the stain.

Above: Left unsealed, brick resists the onslaught of weather season after season. Sealing brick helps prevents stains and darkens the color.

What will it Cost?

Although decks and patios differ in size and scope, these project sketches will give you an idea of what you might pay.

Deck and patio projects are as unique as the people who build them, and each is the result of variables such as property shapes, geographic locations, the position of trees and other important landscape features, the priorities of the homeowners, the kinds of materials used, and the amount of money homeowners are willing to spend to achieve their goals.

Nevertheless, different types of projects have features in common, such as their size and the level of their complexity, that make them useful for approximating costs. In this chapter you'll find illustrations of various deck and patio projects. While each project offers a solution to a specific problem or need, they all serve to expand living space. These deck and patio projects use familiar forms and sizes that the average homeowner might expect to encounter. These vignettes include a few details of construction and approximate costs for materials—as well as estimates of the cost of having a professional contractor complete the job. These estimates, provided by Archadeck, America's largest deck builder, reflect North American averages. You should expect to pay more for materials and labor in more distant locations, such as Honolulu, and lower costs in a less remote locale, where costs of transporting materials are lower.

Use these project estimates to "ballpark" the cost of your own deck and patio. Once planning is underway, get firm estimates from professionals so that your project plans and your budget are in close agreement.

GETTING THE MOST FROM EXISTING SPACE

This walk-out style home had existing outdoor areas—a small, balcony-type porch accessable through a door to the breakfast room, and a large, 32×12-foot, grade-level patio of poured concrete

For general entertaining, however, the porch was too small and the patio was too far away from the main living areas. Adding a 16×12-foot, intermediate-level deck solves the problem. A short stairway leads from the existing porch to the deck, which is positioned so that it won't block daylight from reaching the basement-level patio doors. Another short stairway leads from the deck to the patio.

Underneath the mid-level deck, a 4-foot-high storage space is an added bonus. Lattice panels between the support posts hide stored items, such as extra patio furniture and garden tools, from view. Access to the storage area is provided by hinged panels at the side of the storage area.

To create visual harmony, matching lattice is fastened to 2×4 rails and then fixed between posts to form the railing system. The configuration and placement of the stairways channel traffic away from the main deck area.

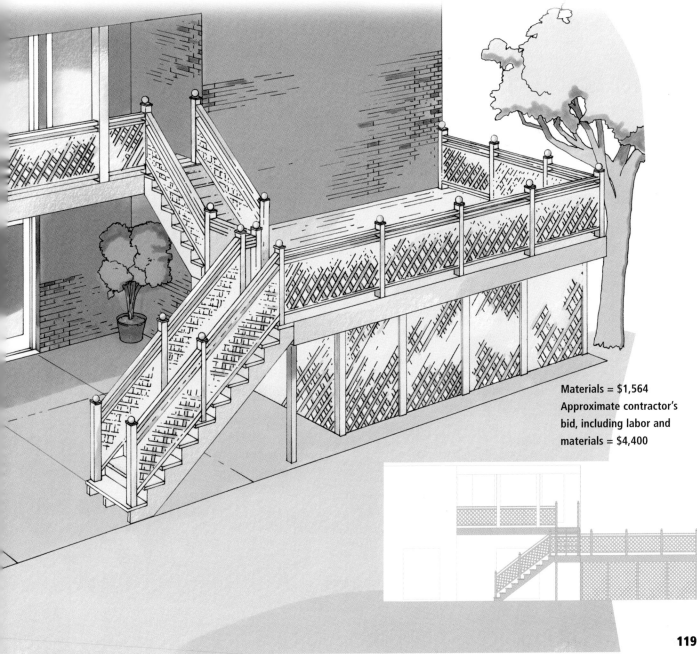

Materials = $1,564
Approximate contractor's
bid, including labor and
materials = $4,400

AN OPEN-AIR ROOM

Materials = $2,592

Approximate contractor's bid, including labor and materials = $5,900

The edges of this all-cedar deck are defined by a simple railing system set between 4×4 posts. To create the illusion of an enclosed room, the posts extend to a height of 7 feet and the tops are connected to each other with 4×4 lumber. This purely decorative touch frames generous "windows" that look out onto the spacious backyard. For visual flair, the decking is laid as concentric squares with mitered corners. The overall look works well with the house, which features rough-sawn cedar siding in a board-and-batten pattern.

Intended as a private deck for the master suite, this configuration would work well as a transitional space from any room. The 16×12-foot dimensions are large enough for entertaining small groups.

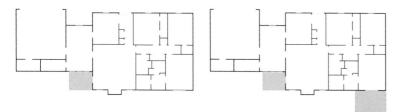

STAYING CONNECTED

This single-story ranch house featured three exterior doors facing the rear of the property, each with a small stoop. By replacing the stoops with a single patio, the three entrances are connected, allowing the homeowners to use different entrances without worrying about tracking dirt. Near the entry to the garage, the patio extends beyond the door to include a storage area for trash cans.

To add a bit of style and visual texture, the concrete patio slab is covered with cut and honed stone tiles. The patio is not large, but it is big enough to allow space for a 4-foot-diameter table, a set of chairs, and a couple of lounge chairs for reading and sunning. The patio steps down 6 inches to a second patio level that measures 15×10 feet and serves as an entryway to the backyard.

Materials = $6,089
Approximate contractor's bid, including labor and materials = $9,000

SLOPE SOLUTION

Materials = $3,850
Approximate contractor's bid, including labor and materials = $10,280

A sloped lot was incorporated into the design of a built-in spa at a back corner of this two-story house, just off an existing mudroom entryway. At the entry, where the lot is level, the homeowners installed a concrete patio with an exposed-aggregate surface. Several feet away, where the lot begins to fall away from the house, an enclosed deck was constructed so that the patio and deck surfaces are flush with each other, creating one large area with different textures. The deck area is the perfect spot for a recessed spa. Doors below the decking provide access to pumps and filters.

To integrate the design, the homeowners chose to enclose the sides of their deck with cedar lap siding that matches the siding of their home. Walls 5 feet high surround the spa area and provide complete privacy. A retaining wall helps stabilize the soils so erosion won't threaten the patio.

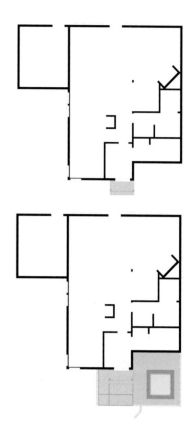

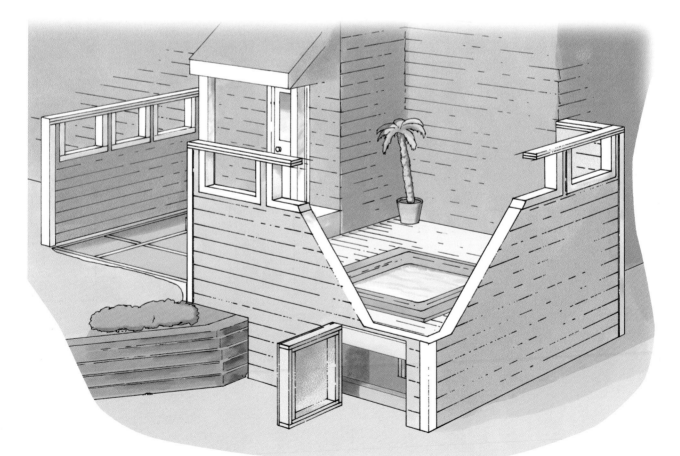

PRESERVING TRADITION

When it came to designing this small, 25×15-foot patio for a two-story, classical-revival brick home, contextual style was important. The owners wanted the space to look as if it had been part of the original design. The solution was to create a sense of quiet dignity that matches the feel of the house. To do that, the landscape architect designed a flat concrete patio with built-in benches supported by concrete-topped brick pillars. The symmetrically arranged benches define the corners of the patio, and the 26-inch-high pillars provide vertical scale that is substantial but not overwhelming. The result is entirely in keeping with the design of the house. The slatted bench seats are made from redwood 2×4s installed on edge. A small, semicircular apron leads from the patio to the backyard.

Materials = $1,967
Approximate contractor's bid, including labor and materials = $3,800

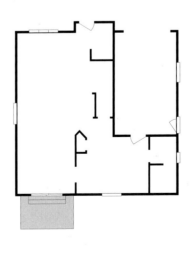

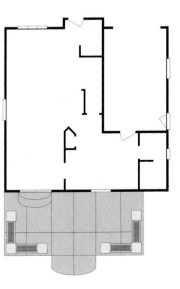

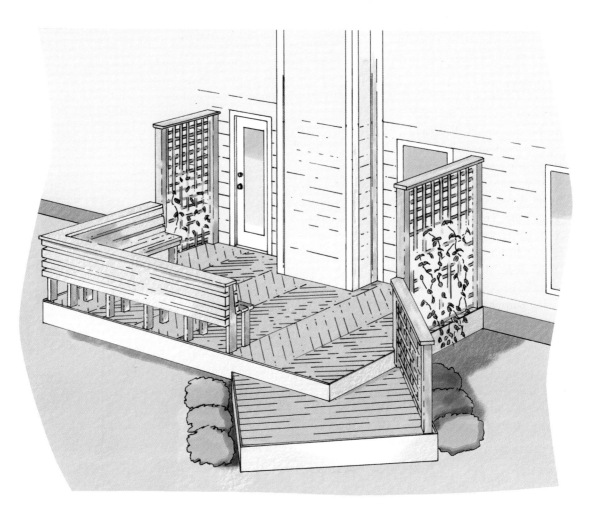

GARDENER'S DELIGHT

To increase their enjoyment of the backyard, the owners of this one-story ranch house added an 18×12-foot deck to the rear of their home. Access is through glass exterior doors that flank the fireplace. The latticework screens on either side of the deck adds to the privacy of the space. The lattice is ideal for climbing greenery, such as clematis or trumpet vine, that enclose the deck with leafy greenery during the growing season. Vines are important to the owners, who have extensive floral gardens and are fond of plants. An 8×8 entry deck completes the design.

While the deck is large enough to hold a small table and a few chairs, bench seating along the perimeter permits entertaining a small group of friends or family without furniture. This platform-style deck is not high enough off the ground to be required by building codes to include a railing, so the bench backs can be normal height. Otherwise, they might be exceptionally tall.

The 1×6 cedar decking is a full 1-inch thick and is laid in a herringbone pattern to create visual interest. The small step deck is set at an angle to add a bit of design flair.

**Materials = $3,480
Approximate contractor's bid, including labor and materials = $8,000**

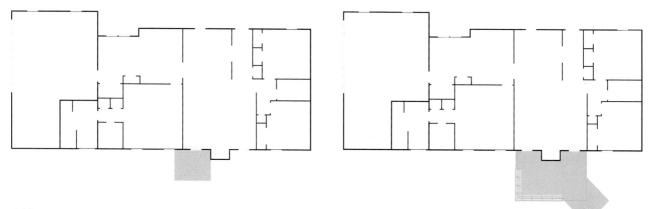

PRIVACY—AN OPEN-AND-SHUT CASE

To get the privacy they wanted, the owners of this single-story home installed a dual-purpose platform deck. One side is completely open and accessible to the house through new patio doors leading from the great room. The other side features a 5-foot-high privacy wall and is accessible to the master bedroom. Two hinged doors, each 2-feet wide, allow the bedroom side of the deck to be opened up or closed. The rear-facing portion of the privacy wall includes a lattice panel that allows air circulation. All-cedar construction is specified, but it would be a good idea to install a vapor barrier in the narrow space between the decking and the ground to help prevent moisture problems. Pressure-treated wood rated for contact with the ground helps prevent damage and extends the life of the deck.

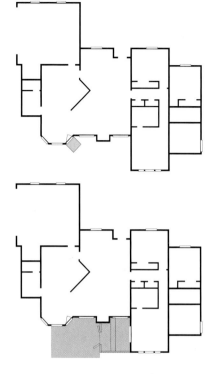

Materials = $2,748
Approximate contractor's bid, including labor and materials = $6,400

SUITE DREAMS

Decks usually are available to main living areas, but the owners of this two-story clapboard home wanted something a bit more unusual—decks for upstairs bedrooms. The basic idea was complicated by a sunny bay window on the lower level that would be covered by a structure overhead.

The solution: Create two small second-level decks—one for the master bedroom and another for the corner bedroom. The plan solves a number of concerns. First, the open space between the decks allows a corridor of daylight to reach the bay. Also, having two small decks avoids the awkward sense of scale that a large, second-level deck and spindly support posts would present. Instead, a handsome stairway visually "grounds" each deck and adds a sense of mass to the vertical supports.

There are also unexpected benefits. The smaller decks create private outdoor suites for lounging and relaxing at treetop level, preserving a sense of privacy and intimacy for the bedrooms. It is relatively simple to install French doors in the exterior walls to create access to the decks.

The plan does not ignore access to main living areas on the lower level. A concrete patio is easily reached through patio doors installed in the bay. Tucked under the twin decks, the patio is naturally divided into smaller "rooms," each providing shifting patterns of sun and shade throughout the day.

Materials = $2,574
Approximate contractor's bid, including labor and materials = $7,700

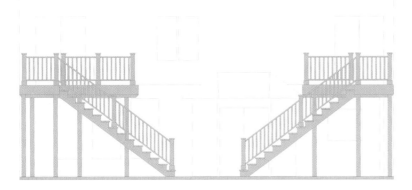

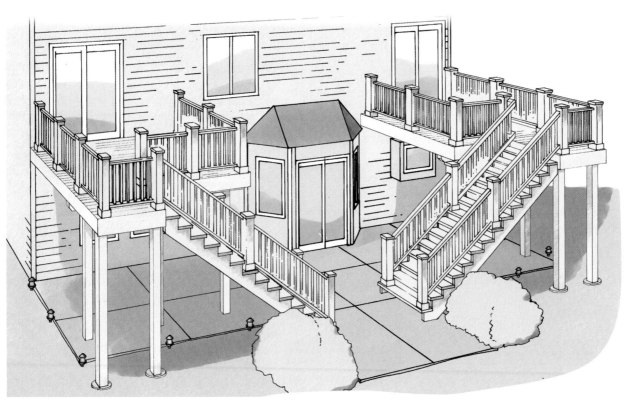

A NEW ANGLE

The back of this two-story house features an L-shaped courtyard where the garage meets the main house. A patio door, set at a 45-degree angle between the garage and main house, and an angled corner to the garage combine to create an unusual configuration of skewed walls. A small, platform-style deck brings all of the elements together and provides a common area connected to the dining room, kitchen, and the master bedroom.

The multilevel deck measures 14 feet across the front edge and 16 feet from the front edge to the main patio doorway. It can be used for entertaining small groups, but it's most used as a point of entry from the backyard. In contrast to the angled walls, the deck has a straightforward, simple design that uses decking installed perpendicular to joists. Built-in planters and short spans of railing add uncomplicated, vertical elements that provide visual interest.

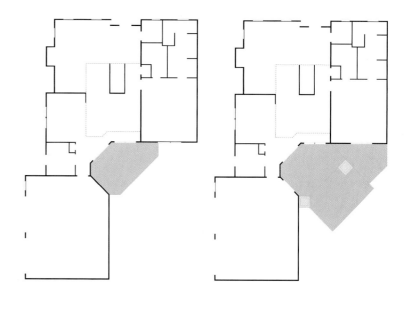

Materials = $1,779
Approximate contractor's bid, including labor and materials = $5,000

Index